"The view that everything can be seen in financial terms is not one shared by everyone. Dr Sandeep Goel in this well-conceived and presented work – across a wide range of capital related issues, provides both a scholarly and practical analysis. Dr Goel's expertise and knowledge – well exhibited in this book, will be of relevance and assistance to so many who professionally or otherwise deal with other people's money."

–**Dr. Barry Rider OBE**, *Professor & Fellow Commoner Emeritus, Jesus College, University of Cambridge, UK*

"A comprehensive and accessible guide to corporate finance, this book skillfully bridges theory and practice. Dr Goel demystifies core financial concepts with clarity, real-world cases, and global relevance. A must-read for business leaders, educators, and students alike seeking sound financial acumen and strategic insight in today's complex economic environment."

– **Dr. Franco Gandolfi**, *Distinguished Professor of Business, California Institute of Advanced Management, Los Angeles, California, USA*

CORPORATE FINANCE

Finance is key to every business organisation and plays a vital role in the broader economic ecosystem. This book discusses the fundamentals of corporate finance and introduces and explains essential concepts of financial management. It delineates the financial workings of businesses in the global context.

The book:

- discusses fundamental concepts and practices of corporate finance;
- demystifies key financial decisions of a corporate: investment decision, financial decision, and dividend decision for shareholders' wealth maximisation;
- highlights the importance of efficient financial management in a corporate enterprise with relevant capital budgeting tools and working capital management techniques; and
- surveys global corporate practices, recent trends, and developments in the domain of business finance. The author addresses the critical issues that a business can face beyond basic survival regarding sound financial management and can help a company grow and thrive.

Presenting current global trends and real-world cases in finance and richly illustrated with tables, figures, and learning tools, this book will be indispensable for individuals, business managers, and management students pursuing courses related to corporate finance and financial management. It will also be an important resource for executive and management development programmes (EDPs & MDPs) as well as professionals and individuals interested in a short refresher course on finance and financial matters.

Sandeep Goel is a Senior Professor of Accounting and Finance, and Corporate Governance at Management Development Institute (MDI) Gurgaon, India. He holds two doctorates, one in Finance; and another in Accounting from the Faculty of Management Studies, University of Delhi. He completed his bachelor's with Hons. and master's degrees in Commerce with specialisation in Finance from Shri Ram College of Commerce and the Department of Commerce, Delhi School of Economics, University of Delhi, respectively. He has three decades of industry and academic experience across various organisations and institutions of repute, including the Shri Ram Group, the University of Delhi, and MDI Gurgaon. He sits as an Independent Director on the Board of Machino Plastics Ltd, Gurugram, a Suzuki JV. He is a Visiting Professor to the Faculty of Management, University of Lodz, Poland, and Aix-Marseille Graduate School of Management, IAE AIX-Marseille University, France. He is a Management Trainer and Consultant to organisations like Maruti Suzuki, Canara Bank, JK Tyre, PFRDA, NPCI, IRS, ITS, FIA Business School (Brazil), Bata, Encore, Federal-Mogul Goetze (India) Ltd, SOS Village International, Cairns India, National Banking Institute (Nepal), Druk Holdings (Bhutan), UltraTech Cements, ONGC, and many more. He is a prolific Writer and has authored more than 15 books and published over 100 research articles and cases in national and international journals of repute. He has been conferred with Award for Excellence in Teaching, 2023–2024, 2015–2016 and Award for Excellence in Research, 2015–2016 at MDI.

Foundations of Finance

Series author: **Sandeep Goel** is a Senior Professor of Accounting and Finance, and Corporate Governance, Management Development Institute (MDI) Gurgaon, India.

This series presents the foundations of financial knowledge in a lucid and accessible format. The books in the series deal with critical themes in financial literacy and proficiency today, such as financial accounting, cost accounting, corporate finance, contemporary finance, forensic accounting, fraud analytics, and fraud risk management. Each volume in the series deals with updated expert insights, current global trends, and real-world cases in finance and is richly illustrated with tables, figures, and learning tools. The individual books in the series will be indispensable for individuals, business managers, and management students pursuing undergraduate and postgraduate courses in finance. They will also be important resources for executive and management development programmes (EDPs & MDPs) as well as beginners and professionals interested in a short refresher course on finance and financial management.

Corporate Finance

Sandeep Goel

CORPORATE FINANCE

Sandeep Goel

Routledge
Taylor & Francis Group
LONDON AND NEW YORK

Designed cover image: Getty Images

First published 2026
by Routledge
4 Park Square, Milton Park, Abingdon, Oxon OX14 4RN

and by Routledge
605 Third Avenue, New York, NY 10158

Routledge is an imprint of the Taylor & Francis Group, an informa business

British Library Cataloguing-in-Publication Data
A catalogue record for this book is available from the British Library

ISBN: 978-1-041-21225-6 (hbk)
ISBN: 978-1-041-22010-7 (pbk)
ISBN: 978-1-003-73016-3 (ebk)

DOI: 10.4324/9781003730163

Typeset in Sabon
by Deanta Global Publishing Services, Chennai, India

CONTENTS

FIGURES

TABLES

PREFACE

Understanding your business's financial health is the fundamental aspect of managerial decision-making and control. A good finance manager is one who is able to (1) invest wisely and timely to avoid various risks, (2) raise funds adequately, and (3) make the right choices about the distribution of profits to shareholders. This is where 'corporate financial efficiency' becomes essential at all levels and in all types of businesses across the globe. This edition is a complete manual on the fundamentals of corporate finance with integral concepts and current trends.

Objectives

The book will help in learning the basic concepts of financial management and enable the managers to use it as an effective tool for financial decision-making and resource allocation.

It helps to answer questions like:

- What is the nitty-gritty involved in financial choices, such as launching a new product, buying a new asset, acquiring another company, and financing the firm's investments?
- How should the firm be managed to increase the wealth of shareholders?
- What decisions must managers make to manage the business operations for sound financial management?

Features

Various aids like figures, tables, illustrations, and case studies have been included in the book on corporate finance to facilitate value addition. The cases of real-world corporate organisations have been analysed and discussed from different sectors. These companies operate internationally, so they will be of immense use to readers worldwide. All these features will make the book more engaging and beneficial to readers.

Organisation of the Book

The book has been divided into five parts. It has been logically sequenced to facilitate better connectivity and learning among the readers. Most chapters are self-contained and can be read independently of the others.

Part I, 'Corporate Finance', is introductory, discussing the financial management process of a business organisation. It demonstrates how managers should make sound financial decisions to maximise the firm's value.

Part II, 'Investment Decision: Capital Budgeting', builds on the time value concepts of compounding and discounting and covers the premise of cash flows estimation, and the key areas of capital investment decision-making with the help of financial tools.

Part III, 'Investment Decision: Working Capital', explains the nuances of working capital management in detail.

Part IV, 'Financing Decision', is a complete description of the funding policies of corporate organizations.

Part V, 'Dividend Decision', elaborates on the dividend distribution policy of corporations for shareholders' wealth maximization (SWM).

This book will build up your finance acumen, which is essential for your professional growth and success. This is a perfect blend of theory with practice. An attempt has been made to keep the book simple in nature yet comprehensive in approach.

I am confident that the readers will find this book truly valuable in terms of its quality and presentation. Any constructive comments and suggestions for future improvement of the book are highly appreciated and welcome at *sandeepgoel1810@gmail.com*.

Happy learning!

ACKNOWLEDGEMENTS

I wish to thank God Almighty for everything in life! The work would be incomplete if I do not acknowledge my parents' contribution. They have been a constant source of inspiration for me and have always stood by me through thick and thin. My wife provided her unstinted support and encouragement in completing the book. My daughter Maanya is my soul whose smile always keeps me going in life.

I am also thankful to the entire team of Routledge, New Delhi, including Dr Shashank Sinha, Mr Yogesh Srivastava, and Ms Anvitaa Bajaj for their tremendous support and wholehearted cooperation at all stages of publication of this book.

My sincere thanks are also due to thank Professor Barry Rider and Professor Franco Gandolfi for their valuable support and endorsements to the book.

Last, but not the least, I gratefully express my gratitude to the following fellow academic colleagues and professional associates for providing their invaluable advice and inputs for the enrichment of the book.

- **Dr Brian P. Miller,** *Professor of Accounting, Warrington College of Business, University of Florida, US*
- **Dr Robert C. Rickards,** *Professor of Accounting, German Police University, Münster, Germany*
- **Dr Maciej Turała,** *Vice Dean for International Relations, University of Lodz, Poland*

- **Mr S. S. Sharma,** *IAS Retd, Former Secretary, Government of India, Gurugram*
- **Dr J. P. Singh,** *Former Professor of Finance, Department of Management Studies, Indian Institute of Technology Roorkee*
- **Mr Aditya Jindal,** *Chairman cum Managing Director, Machino Plastics Ltd, Gurugram*
- **Dr Niti Nandini Chatnani,** *Professor of Finance, Indian Institute of Foreign Trade, New Delhi*
- **Dr Sonam Chawla,** *Associate Professor of Organizational Behaviour, O. P. Jindal Global University, Sonipat*
- **Dr Vishakha Bansal,** *Assistant Professor of Finance & Control, Indian Institute of Management Shillong*
- **Dr Ajay Kumar,** *Assistant Professor, Bharati Vidyapeeth Institute of Management & Research, New Delhi*

ABBREVIATIONS

ARR	Accounting rate of return
BV	Book value per share
CA/FA	Current assets/fixed assets ratio
COCE	Cost of capital employed
CWIP	Capital work in progress
DCF	Discounted cash flow
D / E	Debt–equity ratio
DFL	Degree of financial leverage
DOL	Degree of operating leverage
D / P	Dividend pay-out ratio
DPS	Dividend per share
FV	Future value
IRR	Internal rate of return
MNC	Multinational corporations
MSIL	Maruti Suzuki India Ltd
MV	Market value
NIM	New issue market
NOPAT	Net operating profit after tax
NPV	Net present value
PBDT	Profit before depreciation and tax
PBP	Payback period
PI	Profitability index

PV	Present value
SEBI	Securities and Exchange Board of India
TVM	Time value of money
WACC	Weighted average cost of capital
WCTR	Working capital turnover ratio

PART I

Introduction

1

CORPORATE FINANCE

Nature & Scope

Almost everything in life eventually boils down to the rupee sign. Money, and therefore, finance, is an integral part of life.[1] It applies to business organisations equally. Effective corporate finance is essential to a company's success. In order to produce returns, they must make sure that sufficient funds are available when needed and are allocated to the appropriate projects. Therefore, every business enterprise needs to closely watch the management of its finances.

What Is Corporate Finance?

Corporate finance or 'financial management' *(as commonly called)* is the process of acquisition, allocation, and disbursement of funds. It includes all the activities relating to planning, organising, directing, and controlling the funds of the enterprise.

Elements

1. **Investment Decision:** It implies the allocation of funds into various assets of an undertaking. The investment in fixed assets is called *capital budgeting decision,* and the investment in current assets is called *working capital decision.*
2. **Financing Decision:** It refers to the process of raising funds from various sources depending on factors, such as cost of funds, control, liquidity, and so forth.

DOI: 10.4324/9781003730163-2

3. **Dividend Decision:** This decision involves the distribution of net profit of a business. The management decides what percentage of profits would be distributed as dividend to shareholders and how much profit to be kept aside as reserves for future contingencies.

Objectives of Financial Management

The main objectives of financial management are:

1. **Profit Maximisation:** It is the core objective of financial management. Every business enterprise strives to maximise its profits, both in the short term and the long term.
2. **Wealth Maximisation:** Shareholders' value maximisation is the key objective of financial management and *is preferred over profit maximisation on account of market interest.* Wealth maximisation is a combination of regular return to shareholders in the form of dividend and appreciating market returns.
3. **Liquidity:** Liquidity maintenance is one of the most important objectives of financial management. The firm must have a sound cash position for meeting day-to-day expenses; otherwise, there might be a threat to the survival of the firm.
4. **Solvency:** Long-term soundness is another key objective of financial management. The company must be sound enough to pay interest on long-term loans and repay these loans at regular intervals. Lack of solvency can be a big blow to the firm in the competitive scenario.

Functions of Financial Management

Following are the main functions of financial management:

1. **Forecasting Financial Requirements:** Financial management has to correctly estimate the financial requirements of the business, keeping in view its current operations and future growth.

2. **Acquisition of Funds:** Funds acquisition is another important function of financial management. After estimating the financial requirements, the finance manager has to raise funds from various sources of finance, such as equity, debt, bank loans, and so forth. The optimum capital mix must be maintained.
3. **Proper Allocation of Finance:** The next task of the finance manager is to efficiently allocate these funds according to the nature of assets. Long-term funds should be invested in fixed assets, and short-term funds should be invested in current assets.
4. **Distribution of Profits:** The distribution of net profit of the business is the most important function of finance management as it is oriented towards shareholders' interests. It has to judiciously plan out dividend payment and reinvestment of earnings.
5. **Working Capital Management:** The finance manager must ensure adequate liquidity. He should ensure that enough cash is available for meeting various requirements of the firm, such as payment of salaries, bills, meeting current liabilities, and so forth.
6. **Financial Control:** Sound financial control is the prerequisite for the growth of business. The finance manager must exercise proper control with the help of techniques like budgetary control, cost analysis, financial forecasting, and so forth.

Corporate Finance Scenario in India

Traditionally, a single manager would manage the entire operations of the business. With the business becoming globalised, the finance function has become a specialised function. There are finance specialists now to manage your operations.

Since liberalisation in 1991, the Indian corporate sector has changed tremendously in its form and working, making finance the most sophisticated function of corporate enterprise. There are specialist groups of executives in companies today, managing the finance function, called director-finance, chief finance officer, and financial controller.

The finance manager is not merely concerned with maintaining accounts of the business. He has to perform multiple tasks, including fundraising, procurement of assets, distribution of profits, and ensuring the safety of the financial assets of the company. He has to plan out the operations of a business in such a manner so that both continuity and growth of the business are maintained at the same time. He is expected to generate maximum profits for the company and keep shareholders satisfied.

The financial management is continuously progressing. A good finance manager must see all updates and changes in the field of financial management and implement them accordingly. He should be interested to know what new sources of funds are developed at an international level, what new projects are there, and what amendments are made by the government in various laws. In short, a good finance manager must be aware of what is happening around.

CONTROLLER'S AND TREASURER'S FUNCTIONS IN THE INDIAN CONTEXT

The 'controller' and 'treasurer' are essentially American terms. However, this pattern is not being widely followed in India. There are companies in India that have designations of the controller or the financial controller.

The 'controller' or the financial controller in India performs the functions of a chief accountant or management accountant. The officer with the title of 'treasurer' can also be found in a few companies in India. However, in most cases, as mentioned above in the case of Indian companies, the terms like general manager (finance) or vice-president (finance) are more popular.

Some of the functions of the controller and the treasurer, such as *government reporting, insurance management, and so forth,* are taken care of by the company secretary in India. In the American business, the management of finance is treated as a separate activity and is performed by the treasurer.

Following are the main changes that have tuned the field of financial management in India during the last few decades:

1. **Interest Rates:** The interest rates are controlled by the RBI and thus, commercial banks' rates are affected by the RBI's action. This has an important bearing on the cost of debt.
2. **Valuation of Shares:** The value of shares can now be determined at a premium or discount freely. One should determine their share value at an optimum level because it directly affects the EPS.
3. **Mergers and Acquisitions:** A good finance manager should keep his eye on who is taking over which company. To merge with another company may sometimes be more profitable than going alone.

In conclusion, financial management has evolved with the times and become scientific with the latest principles and practices of management.

Financial Management Problems

The common problems relating to the financial management faced by corporate enterprises are discussed below:

1. **Lack of an Optimum Source of Funds:** Due to poor planning, the enterprises *do not maintain a desirable combination of sources of funds*. This leads to a shortage of equity and then they depend too much on borrowed capital. Hence, sound financial planning is required for an optimal financial structure.
2. **Inadequate Combination of Assets:** This results in the problem of either shortage or excess of assets for the business. This is more pertinent to current assets, such as inventories and receivables. For a manufacturing undertaking, these problems need an immediate check by adopting appropriate working capital techniques.

3. **Inaccurate Projection of Revenue and Cost:** This results in improper investment in inventories, receivables, and plant capacity. These factors ultimately result in poor earnings of the enterprise. So, there should be an efficient and effective profit planning for better utilisation of resources and enhanced earnings.
4. **Absence of Stable Dividend Policy:** In the absence of a definite and stable dividend policy, the shareholders withdraw from the company. So, there should be a sound dividend policy, and dividend payments should be regular and consistent in proportion to the paid-up capital.
5. **Unprofessional Management:** If there is incompetent management, it leads to instability in the organisation. The enterprise should be managed by *professionally competent, qualified,* and *experienced personnel* for better results orientation.

Reference

1. Emery, Douglas R., et al. 1998. *Principles of Financial Management.* Englewood Cliffs, NJ: Prentice Hall, p. 2.

PART II

Investment Decision

A. Capital Budgeting

2

CAPITAL BUDGETING

Concept and application

The capital budgeting decision refers to the investment in long-term assets. *Capital budgeting is often used interchangeably with terms like 'capital expenditure' (capex) or capital investment*. A capital budgeting decision is considered to be final since it entails significant financial commitments and a high level of risk regarding the company's ability to generate future returns. For the project to be successful, a thorough analysis and evaluation of the suggested capital budgeting decision are therefore necessary. To ascertain which projects will provide the highest return over a specified time frame, capital budgeting techniques must be applied.

Meaning of Capital Budgeting

The capital budgeting decision refers to the investment in a fixed asset whose returns are expected over a long period of time. 'It is the process of identifying, analysing and selecting investment projects whose returns (cash flows) are expected to extend beyond one year'.[1] Thus, any expenditure that generates a cash flow benefit for more than one year is capital expenditure. *For example*, the purchase of a new machine, acquiring another company, research and development, and so forth.

DOI: 10.4324/9781003730163-4

TYPES OF CAPITAL BUDGETING DECISIONS

The capital investment decisions are classified as follows:

1. **Replacement Decision**: It is the most routine decision of an undertaking which involves the decision of replacing an old asset with the new asset. This is essential to ensure a smooth level of business operations.
2. **Expansion/modernisation Decision**: This decision is about increasing the production capacity of the business or modernisation of the existing facilities to meet growing demands by introducing new men, machines, or/and methods.
3. **Diversification Decision**: This is deciding to enter into new lines of business either related or unrelated based on the company's growth plans and competitive conditions. Such decisions result in increasing requirements for fixed assets.

The capital investment decision is the most difficult and important decision for the business as it determines the success of an enterprise in the long run.

In a 'capital investment decision', the major criterion for selection of a project is its viability and impact on shareholder value. The two most important parameters for arriving at a project decision are the *project's expected cash inflows* and *cash outflows*. They determine whether the returns meet a sufficient target benchmark or not.

The capital budgeting decision can basically be grouped into:

1. allocation of long-term funds into fixed assets;
2. risk analysis of capital investment decisions; and
3. measurement of the cost of capital.

Capital Budgeting Process

The capital budgeting process consists of the following steps:

1. **Identifying Investment Needs:** The identification of the need for capital investment is the first step. This involves the evaluation of various available opportunities by the management on the basis of both financial and non-financial factors. The key criterion is the 'risk-return trade-off'.
2. **Project Feasibility Study:** The next step is to evaluate the proposal for its feasibility at various levels of *economic viability, commercial viability, technical viability, and financial viability.*
3. **Capital Project Evaluation:** After deciding on the proposed project, its evaluation is done regarding its viability using both qualitative and quantitative methods. The estimated cash flows, target cost of capital, and potential risks are identified for the evaluation. Calculating the appropriate discount rate is a critical part of this process.

   Finally, various capital budgeting techniques are applied to test their feasibility (discussed later in the chapter).
4. **Capital Investment Implementation:** Once the proposed project is deemed viable, the project team executes it.

FACTORS USED FOR THE EVALUATION

1. **Initial Cash Outflows**: It is the amount of cash flow to be invested initially in the project.
2. **Net Cash Inflows from Operations**: It is the amount of cash inflows to be generated from the capital investment decision.
3. **Terminal Cash Flows**: It is the 'salvage value' (residual value) of an existing asset at the end of its life.
4. **Depreciation**: The usage charge of an asset.
5. **Income Tax Effect**: Tax shield on account of sale of an asset.
6. **Discounting Rate**: The funding rate in the computation of cash flows.
7. **Risk Factor(s)**: Political risk, monetary risk, and other risks should be considered in the evaluation process.

Capital Budgeting Projects

The capital investment projects are categorised as follows:

1. **Independent Projects:** These are the projects whose selection does not affect the selection of any other project, i.e., they are independent of other projects. *For example, you have Rs. 50,000. You decide to buy a water purifier that costs about Rs. 10,000 and a new laptop for your house that costs around Rs. 20,000. The decision to buy the purifier does not affect the decision to buy the laptop – they are independent decisions.*
2. **Dependent Projects or Contingent Projects:** The acceptance of these projects is dependent upon the acceptance of other projects. *For example, procurement of furniture due to the construction of a new office is a case of a dependent project. Here, the usage of new furniture is dependent upon the new office.*
3. **Mutually Exclusive Projects:** These projects are ones where the investment in one project affects other projects because only one project can be undertaken. *Taking the first example further, let us assume that you have decided to buy only a water purifier. You looked at two different brands of purifiers, one is A and the other is B. So, when you decide to buy B, you have also decided you are not going to buy A.*

Project Feasibility

Project feasibility or project appraisal is 'assessing, in advance, whether a project is viable to be undertaken or not'. Therefore, before deciding on a project, one must evaluate its 'feasibility'. *The feasibility study can be conducted for smaller projects as well, but generally on account of time and effort involved, it is conducted more often for bigger projects.*[2]

> A *feasible capital project* is one which generates adequate operating cash inflows, withstands all the risks and lasts for its predetermined life to meet the desired goals.

Types of Project Feasibility

Following types of feasibility studies are conducted to analyse the viability of a project:

Market Feasibility

The *market feasibility* is helpful in identifying the business opportunities for the proposed project. Based on the opportunities found, the project should proceed further.

This analysis uses several tools to determine feasibility:

1. **Demographic Analysis**: This involves analysis of demographic trends that are occurring in a particular market area, based on indicators like age, education, and income level. The demographic analysis is helpful in providing key inferences on demand changes occurring in the market.
2. **Industry Analysis**: This analysis examines and identifies industries trends that are presently occurring in the marketplace and thereby helps in identifying what industries are most appropriate for the area by estimating industry supply and industry competition.
3. **Retail Sales Analysis**: Retail sales analysis focuses on purchasing trends of the existing population within a market area and whether there is an opportunity for new retail to capture a portion of the existing market.

Technical Feasibility

Technical feasibility enables the determination of the technical requirements of men, machines, and materials of the proposed project. Accordingly, the organisation finds out whether it has sufficient technical resources to undertake the project or not. It may consider taking help from outside if there is a lack of internal technical know-how.

The tools used to determine technical feasibility are:

1. **Technology Analysis**: This is assessing the type of technology required for the project and the constraints involved in the implementation. Thus, it determines the reliability and competitiveness of technology for the project.
2. **Resource Analysis**: Based on the technology, the requirement of men, materials, and other inputs needed to produce a product or service are listed. This provides information about the operations of your business.
3. **Environmental Analysis**: This consists of analysing the environmental impacts of the business. It evaluates the category of business with its potential impact on traffic, water reserves, and other significant natural resources.

Economic Feasibility

The *economic feasibility* is the baseline of any feasibility study as this determines the commercial viability of the project. A project is considered to be economically feasible if its probable revenues exceed the total costs. This assessment typically involves a 'cost-benefit analysis' of the project based on which necessary financial resources are allocated.

The following techniques are used to determine the economic feasibility:

1. **Cost Analysis**: This analysis determines the possible cost structure of the project. Questions about operating and other related costs are answered at this stage for determining the economic viability of the project.

2. **Revenue Analysis**: In order to ensure the success of a project, you need to know your business will make profits. Therefore, 'revenue projection' is done to find out the expected revenue, profit margin, and expected net profit of the project.

Financial Feasibility

The *financial feasibility* is the most important part of any feasibility study as this determines the funding requirement of the project. A project is considered to be financially feasible if its probable cost of finance is lowest at a given level of profits.

The following appraisal is used to determine the financial feasibility:

1. **Capital Analysis**: This provides information about the funds required to start the project and keep it running until it is self-sustaining. You should include enough capital funds to run the business.

Organisational Feasibility

The *organisational or managerial feasibility* aims at determining the managerial capability to undertake the project. The most viable projects on all parameters fail at times due to incompetent management.

This applies the following tools:

1. **Organisation Structure Analysis**: This study identifies the proposed legal structure of the business with all the stakeholders involved. The availability of skilled and experienced business managers is identified to ensure the professional handling of the project.
2. **Performance Analysis**: The formal review process of the project with all parties involved at periodic intervals is necessary for achieving the desired results of the project. The review fixes the responsibility of individuals for the job.

Capital Investment Analysis of DLF and Unitech

The analysis of capital budgeting practices of two major players in the Indian realty sector, namely, DLF Ltd and Unitech Ltd is discussed below.

Indian Realty Sector

The real estate sector in India is one of the most globally recognised sectors and is the second largest employer after agriculture. *DLF* has over 75 years of track record of sustained growth and its primary business is the development of residential, commercial, and retail properties. *Unitech*, established in 1971, is today a leading real estate developer in India. *These companies have a global presence. Therefore, the analysis of their capital investment practices will be useful worldwide. The data has been taken from the annual reports of companies.*

Investment Pattern

The trend of investment in long-term assets (*fixed assets/non-current assets*) of the units is analysed to find out whether they are growing or not. It is further evaluated to determine the risk strategy of the management in the environment within which they operate.

DLF Ltd

The investments of DLF for four years as on March 31 are given in Table 2.1.

It is clear that the investments by DLF have been increasing every year till 2021, indicating a growing trend (see Figure 2.1). DLF unlocked about Rs. 2,734 crores during 2021–2022 by divesting certain non-core assets and businesses. This implies that more funds could be realised through divestments over the

TABLE 2.1 Investment pattern of DLF

Year	*2019*	*2020*	*2021*	*2022*
Investments (Rs. in crores)	16,919.08	20,875.91	27,448.03	24,714.81

Note: Rs. 1 crore = Rs. 10 million.

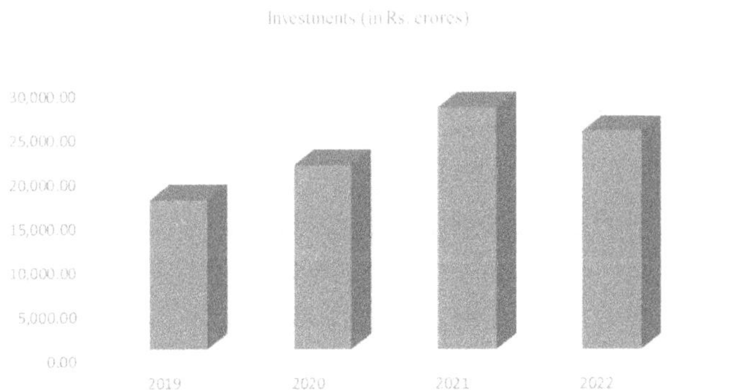

FIGURE 2.1 Investment trend of DLF

next couple of years. The cash flow from divestment would be utilised primarily for debt reduction.

Unitech Ltd

The investments of Unitech for a span of four years as on March 31 are given in Table 2.2.

As it can be seen from the data that the company's investments showed an opposite trend as compared to DLF (see Figure 2.2). It has been continuously declining till 2021 and has increased marginally since then. The company is exposed to specific risks in connection with the management of investments and the environmental uncertainties. The company needs to measure and

TABLE 2.2 Investment pattern of Unitech

Year	*2019*	*2020*	*2021*	*2022*
Investments (Rs. in crores)	2,787.72	2,511.05	1,625.80	1,631.52

Note: Rs. 1 crore = Rs. 10 million.

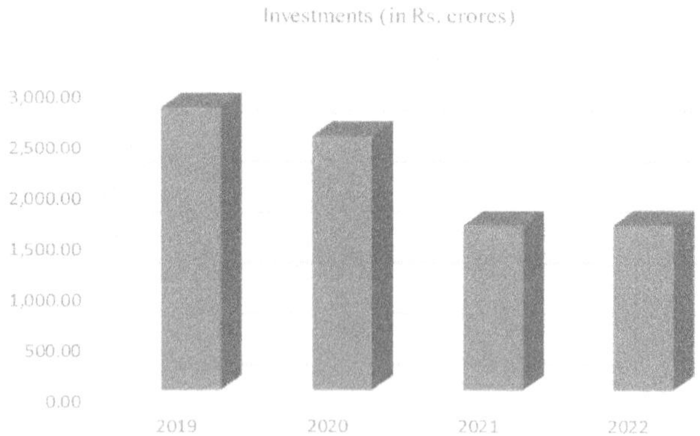

FIGURE 2.2 Investment trend of Unitech

monitor these risks and ensure that it adheres to the policies and procedures for mitigating them and plans its investments well for future growth.

Operating Risk

Operating risk indicates the resources' sufficiency for the required growth of business units. To measure the degree of operating risk, the 'current assets/fixed assets' (CA/FA) ratio has been used, as it determines the availability of resources to the business according to the nature of industry.

DLF Ltd

The composition of total assets of DLF for the time period is given in Table 2.3.

The 'current assets to fixed assets ratio' is above 1 during the first two years, meaning the company's operating risk is on a much higher side, reflecting too high current assets despite the captive nature of the industry. But, since 2021, it is quite satisfactory. It does have adequate capital resources to support its growth.

TABLE 2.3 Assets composition of DLF

	March 2019	*March 2020*	*March 2021*	*March 2022*
Current assets (Rs. in crores)	18,078.18	21,287.43	12,625.75	12,600.85
Fixed assets (Rs. in crores)	16,919.08	20,875.91	27,448.03	24,714.81
Current assets to fixed assets ratio (times)	1.07	1.02	0.46	0.51

Note: Rs. 1 crore = Rs. 10 million.

TABLE 2.4 Assets composition of Unitech

Ratio	*Mar 2019*	*March 2020*	*March 2021*	*March 2022*
Current assets (Rs. in crores)	16,778.19	15,057.10	15,136.62	15,358.01
Fixed assets (Rs. in crores)	2,787.72	2,511.05	1,625.80	1,631.52
Current assets to fixed assets ratio (times)	6.02	6	9.31	9.41

Note: Rs. 1 crore = Rs. 10 million.

Unitech Ltd

The composition of total assets of Unitech for the time period is given in Table 2.4.

The 'current to fixed asset ratio' is very high, meaning the company's current resources are much greater than the required norm of 40:60 (current assets:fixed assets) average of the construction industry. In contrast, the capital resources to fund the business growth are quite low and signal a high level of operating risk, particularly in 2021 and 2022.

References

1. Van Horne, James C., et al. 1996. *Fundamentals of Financial Management*, Ninth Edition. New Delhi: Prentice-Hall of India Private Limited, p. 314.
2. Goel, Sandeep. 2015. *Capital Budgeting*. New York: Business Expert Press, p. 19.

3

TIME VALUE OF MONEY

The time value of money (TVM) is the foundational concept in capital budgeting decisions. Its main purpose is to compare different investment options for the current purchasing power of money. The time value of money should be appropriately taken into account when making capital budgeting decisions; otherwise, failing to do so would make the capital budgeting analysis impracticable.

What Is Time Value of Money?

Time value of money describes the relationship between the 'value of rupee today' and 'value of rupee in future'. It refers to the purchasing power of money exercised by an individual with the changing times.[1] TVM is based on the concept that a rupee that you have today is worth more than the promise or expectation that you will receive a rupee in the future. The money held today is more valuable because you can invest it and earn interest.

For instance, you can invest your rupee for one year at a 7% annual interest rate and accumulate Rs. 1.07 at the end of the year. The *future value* of the rupee after one year is Rs. 1.07 at 7% interest rate and the *present value* of Rs. 1.07 to be received at the end of one year is only Rs. 1. This example is illustrated in the following figure (Figure 3.1).

DOI: 10.4324/9781003730163-5

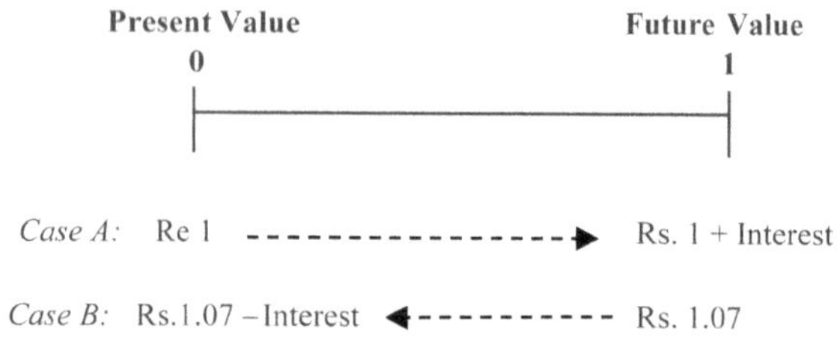

FIGURE 3.1 TVM principle

> **THE MONEY HAS TIME PREFERENCE ON ACCOUNT OF THE FOLLOWING KEY FACTORS:**
>
> 1. Risk/uncertainty
> 2. Preference for consumption
> 3. Investment opportunities.[2]

Methods of Valuation

The two methods of accounting used for the time value of money are compounding and discounting. *Compounding* denotes the future value of a present sum of money. *Discounting* implies the present value of a future sum of money.

Compounding – 'Future Value' (FV)

Future Value of an Amount of Rupee

$$FV(A) = P \times (1 + r) \tag{3.1}$$

Here, A = Future value of the lump sum at the end of the period
P = Amount invested today
r = Interest rate

Illustration 3.1: Mr Jack decides to invest Rs. 5,000 in a fixed deposit account at an annual interest rate of 7%. What is the compounded value after 5 years?

Solution

$$\begin{aligned} A\ (FV) &= P\ (1 + r)^n \\ \text{So, } A &= \text{Rs. } 5{,}000\ (1 + .07)^5 \\ &= \text{Rs. } 5{,}000 \times 1.403^* \\ &= \text{Rs. } 7{,}015 \end{aligned} \tag{3.2}$$

Hence, the compounded value of Rs. 5,000 will be Rs. 7,015.

Note*: Using compound value of Re. 1 table, we get the 'compound value factor' of Re. 1 at 7% per annum at the end of 5 years as 1.403.

Excel Function to Find 'Future Value'

FORMULA: FV (RATE, NPER, PMT, PV, TYPE)

FV = Future Value
RATE = Interest rate per period (year, month, day, etc.)
NPER = Total number of periods
PV = Present value (mark it negative as it is an outflow)

PMT and TYPE are used in case of annuities

PMT variable denotes a series of payments at equal intervals.

TYPE variable tells whether the cash flow occurs at the end (0) or in the beginning (1) of the period.

In order to use this function and other financial functions,

1. Open an Excel sheet.
2. Go to Functions, *fx* below the Menu bar.
3. Under the fx, select a category of 'Financial'.
   (There will be various classifications like Math & Trig/ Statistical/Logical, etc.)

Now, in the above example, principal is Rs. 5,000, 5 years period and the rate of interest is 7%.

Enter = FV(B3, B4, B5, –B2, B6)

The result is 7,013, which we approximately got manually as well (Exhibit 3.1).

Exhibit 3.1

	A	B
1	FUTURE VALUE CALCULATIONS	
2	PRESENT VALUE	5,000
3	RATE	7%
4	YEARS (NPER)	5
5	PAYMENTS MADE (PMT)	0
6	TYPE	0
7	FUTURE VALUE	7,013

Note: The same function can be experimented/applied with different values in the same function and the result will be updated in Cell No. B7.

Future Value of an Annuity Series of Cash Flows

If the same amount is invested every year, it is termed an 'annuity'.

$$A(FV) = P\left[\frac{(1+r)^n - 1}{r}\right] \tag{3.3}$$

Here, A = Future value of the annuity at the end of the period

P = Amount invested at regular intervals

r = Annual rate of interest

n = Number of years of annuity

Illustration 3.2: Mr Mac plans to buy an equipment after three years. He plans to deposit Rs. 2,000 at the end of each year into a bank savings account paying a fixed rate of interest of 7%. How much will he get after three years?

Solution

$$A(FV) = P\left[\frac{(1+r)^n - 1}{r}\right]$$

$$A(FV) = 2{,}000\left[\frac{(1+0.07)^3 - 1}{0.07}\right]$$

$$\begin{aligned}\text{So, A} &= \text{Rs. } 2{,}000 \times 3.215^{*} \\ &= \text{Rs. } 6{,}430\end{aligned} \tag{3.4}$$

Note*: Using compound value annuity tables, we get the compound value factor of Re. 1 at 7% per annum at the end of three years as 3.2.

Excel Function to Find 'Future Value of Annuity'

FORMULA: FV (RATE, NPER, PMT, PV, TYPE)

In case of Annuity:

- PV will be zero.
- PMT will be negative as payment made. TYPE is also to be used.

Using the same formula as in point 1 above, with payments made (uniform) of Rs. 2,000, 3 years period, and 7% rate of interest,

Enter = FV(B3, B4,–B5, B2, B6)

The result is 6,430, which we got manually as well (Exhibit 3.2).

Exhibit 3.2

	A	*B*
1	FUTURE VALUE OF ANNUITY CALCULATIONS	
2	PRESENT VALUE	0
3	RATE	7%
4	YEARS (NPER)	3
5	PAYMENTS MADE (PMT)	2000
6	TYPE	0
7	FUTURE VALUE	6,430

Note: The same function can be experimented/applied with different values in the same function and the result will be updated in Cell No. B7.

INTEREST RATE DETERMINATION

The present or future value of cash inflows is calculated using an interest rate or discount rate (also known as 'cost of capital'). This rate is determined on the basis of various factors, such as:

1. **Inflation rate**: The higher the inflation rate, the higher the return expected by the investors on their investment.
2. **Interest rate**: The higher the interest rate on deposits, the greater the loss of interest income on future cash inflows leading to demand for higher returns on investment by the investors.
3. **Risk premium**: The higher the risk of a project, the higher the return expectations of an investor.

Discounting – 'Present Value' (PV)

Present Value of a Future Amount

$$PV(P) = \frac{A}{(1+r)} \tag{3.5}$$

Here, P = Present value of the lump sum today
A = Amount received a year after
r = Interest rate

Illustration 3.3: Mr Ravi aspires to receive Rs. 1,000 after three years at the rate of 8%. What is the present value of future cash inflows?

Solution

$$PV = \left[\frac{A}{(1+r)^n}\right] \tag{3.6}$$

So,

$$PV = \left[\frac{1{,}000}{(1+0.08)^3}\right]$$

$$= \text{Rs.}\,1{,}000 \times 0.794^{*} \tag{3.7}$$

$$= \text{Rs.}\,794$$

Hence, the present value of Rs. 1,000 will be Rs. 794.

Note*: Using present value tables, we get the present value factor of Re. 1 at 8% per annum at the end of three years as 0.794.

Excel Function to Find 'Present Value'

FORMULA: PV (RATE, NPER, PMT, FV, TYPE)

PV = Present value
RATE = Interest rate per period (year, month, day, etc.)
NPER = Total number of periods
FV = Future value

PMT and TYPE, as mentioned in *FV* discussion, are used in case of annuities.

Repeating the above EXCEL process in illustration 12.3, to get Rs. 1,000 after 3 years at 8% rate of interest we get:

Enter = PV(B3, B4, B5, B2, B6)

The result is –794 (outflow) to be made to receive Rs. 1,000 after 3 years. This we got manually as well (Exhibit 3.3).

Exhibit 3.3

	A	B
1	PRESENT VALUE CALCULATIONS	
2	FUTURE VALUE	1,000
3	RATE	8%
4	YEARS (NPER)	3
5	PAYMENTS (PMT)	0
6	TYPE	0
7	PRESENT VALUE	–794

Note: The same function can be experimented/applied with different values in the same function and the result will be updated in Cell No. B7.

Excel Function to Find 'Present Value of Annuity'

FORMULA: PV (RATE, NPER, PMT, FV, TYPE)

In case of Annuity:

- FV will be zero
- PMT and TYPE are to be used.

Use the same formula as in point 3 above, with payments/cash flows (uniform) of Rs. 5,000 for a 40-year time period at the 7% discount rate.

Enter = PV(B3, B4, B5, B2, B6)

The result is –66,659 which we almost got manually as well (Exhibit 3.4).

This means that if we invest this amount, we will receive Rs. 5000 for 40 years at the given rate.

Exhibit 3.4

	A	B
1	PRESENT VALUE OF ANNUITY CALCULATIONS	
2	FUTURE VALUE	0
3	RATE	7%
4	YEARS (NPER)	40
5	PAYMENTS (PMT)	5000
6	TYPE	0
7	PRESENT VALUE	-66,659

Note: The same function can be experimented/applied with different values in the same function and the result will be updated in Cell No. B7.

Present Value of an Annuity

In the case of the same amount periodically, it is termed an 'annuity'.

$$PV = A \times \frac{1}{r}\left[1 - \frac{1}{(1+r)^n}\right] \tag{3.8}$$

Here, P/PV = Present value of the instalments today
A = Instalment at the end of each period
r = Rate of discount
n = Number of years of annuity

Illustration 3.4: Mr Amit has won a competition and is expecting to receive Rs. 5,000 at the end of each year for the next 40 years. What is the present value of Rs. 5,000 due to be received at the 7% discount rate?

SolutionTech: The equation below is not visible.

$$PV = \text{A} \times \frac{1}{r}\left[1 - \frac{1}{(1+r)^3}\right]$$

So,

$$= \text{Rs.}5{,}000 \times 13.332^{*} \qquad (3.9)$$

$$= \text{Rs.}66{,}660$$

Hence, solving the equation above, the present value of Rs. 5,000 annuity comes out to be Rs. 66,660.

Note*: Using present value annuity tables, we get the present value factor of annuity of Re. 1 at 7% per annum at the end of 40 years as 13.332.

References

1. Goel, Sandeep. 2015. *Capital Budgeting*. New York: Business Expert Press, p. 47.
2. Goel, Sandeep. 2015. *Capital Budgeting*. New York: Business Expert Press, p. 47.

4

CASH FLOWS ESTIMATION FOR CAPEX

As the capital investment decisions must be made now, not later, they are based on 'cash-flow concepts' as opposed to profit-based concepts. The decision-making process for capital investments is driven by cash flows. When the investment is made in a project, it guides the management for future orientation. Consequently, the accuracy with which cash flows are computed determines whether an investment decision is successful or unsuccessful. Understanding the procedure for calculating cash flows is essential when making capital investment decisions.

How to Estimate Cash Flows?

Cash flow can arise from a revenue or expense stream that changes a cash account over a given period.[1] *Cash inflows* are expected returns from the operating activities, whereas *cash outflows* are an outcome of the investing activities. This process of cash flows determines the liquidity position of the business and its capacity to undertake the required project. Therefore, estimation of cash inflows and outflows correctly is vital for the continued existence and growth of business in future. Incorrect forecasting of cash flows could lead to the acceptance of an unprofitable project or rejection of profitable projects.

DOI: 10.4324/9781003730163-6

> Cash inflows expected from a project are 'after-tax operating cash flows', as the project is supposed to generate cash returns from its core activities and that too after the corporate tax has been provided for. They denote the real return for the shareholders (owners) of the business.

The estimation of future cash flows is not easy for the management due to the uncertainty element of the future. *For example*, in the case of project of similar nature in the past, it is relatively easier to estimate the cash flows for the management than in the case of a completely new project.

The factors given below must be kept in mind while estimating cash flows.

1. *Relevant Cash Flows*

The cash flows considered for capital budgeting decisions should always be 'relevant' cash flows.

Relevant cash flows are determined keeping in view the following factors.

(a) *Sunk costs*

It is a cash outflow associated with the project which has already occurred in the past and will not be affected by the decision to undertake the investment. *For example*, a firm incurs Rs. 50,000 for the ground inspection of the project before any decision about its acceptance or rejection. This amount of Rs. 50,000 will be an outflow irrespective of the final decision. Thus, it is a 'sunk cost'.

This cost should not be included in the capital budgeting analysis because it is not a relevant cash flow for the project decision-making. So, all costs and cash outflows of such nature should not be considered in the capital budgeting decision.

(b) *Incidental capital expenses (commissioning expenses, like transportation and installation costs)*

These costs generally are not included in the purchase price of an asset, but they are essential for using the asset. *For example*, the firm buys an equipment for Rs. 10,000 and spends another Rs. 2,000 on its installation. The additional Rs. 2,000 will be added to the total capital cost of the equipment; that is, the total capital expenditure will be Rs. 12,000.

The depreciable cost of an asset will include the purchase price plus all the commissioning expenses incurred to make the asset operational. In the above case, the depreciation will be charged on Rs. 12,000.

(c) *Inflation*

The inflation factor, as discussed earlier, has an important bearing on the interest rate. Therefore, it should be duly incorporated while estimating the future cash flows associated with a project; otherwise, it might result in a wrong decision.

2. *Incremental Cash Flows*

The next important factor is that cash flows in capital budgeting decisions should always be 'incremental' cash flows associated with the asset. *Incremental* implies the 'net benefit or net advantage'.[2] This means that only those cash flows should be considered which are affected by the capital investment.

The *incremental factor* in cash flows arises due to the concept of 'opportunity cost'.* This implies that every investment decision has at least two alternatives. Let's understand this with the following scenarios:

Scenario 1: Replacement of an old asset

Scenario 2: Investment choice between two projects, Project A or Project B

Scenario 3: Investment in a project or not

In these three scenarios, there is a second alternative available. Even in the third case of investment in a single project, there is a choice available whether to invest or not to invest. So, for rational decision-making, cash flows to be considered for capital investment should be 'incremental cash flows' instead of absolute cash flows.

* Opportunity cost is the next best return sacrificed if the funds are not invested in the proposed capital budgeting project.

Components of Cash Flows (Incremental Cash Flows)

There are three components of cash flows that are required for capital budgeting decisions:

1. *Initial cash outflows/Initial investment*
2. *Annual (average) cash inflows from an investment*
3. *Terminal cash flows (salvage value).*

(i) **Initial Cash Outflows:** This is the investment outlay on the asset which occurs at the beginning of the life of the project. These cash flows include the purchase price of the asset, additional capital expenses, the changes in net working capital, the cash flows from the disposal of the old asset (in case of replacement), and the tax implications.

The item *'changes in net working capital'* refers to the possible change in any item of current asset/current liability (working capital) on account of the capital investment. *For example,* if the new machine improves the production efficiency, thereby consuming less raw material (inventory) as compared to the old machine, this will result in saving cash.

This implies a decrease in working capital, that is, the change in net working capital will be positive and will be deducted from the total cash outflows above and vice versa.

How to Calculate Cash Outflows?

Initial Cash Outflow

Purchase price of new asset(s)/project(s)
+ Incidental capital expenses
(e.g. transportation costs, installation costs, etc.)
+(−) Increase/decrease in net working capital
− Net proceeds from the sale of old asset
+(−) Increase in taxes/tax savings due to the disposal of old asset
(if the investment is a replacement decision)
= Initial cash outflow

Illustration 4.1: Computation of initial cash outflows

Y'N'G Ltd plans to replace their old printing machine. From the following information, calculate the net cash outflow required for such replacement:

Cost of the old machine is Rs. 20,000 with a book value of Rs. 3,000.
Life of the old machine is seven years.
Purchase price of the new machine is Rs. 70,000.
Shipping expenses incurred on its transportation are Rs. 10,000.
Sale proceeds of old machine are Rs. 5,000.
Additional working capital requirement is Rs. 2,000. Corporate tax rate is 25%.

Solution

	Rs.
Cost of the new machine	70,000
Add: Shipping expenses	10,000
Add: Additional working capital required	2,000
Add: Income tax liability (2,000 × 25 / 100)*	500
Less: Sale proceeds of old machine	82,500
	5,000
Net cash outflow	**77,500**

*Profit on sale = Rs. 5,000 – Rs. 3,000 = Rs. 2,000

(ii) **Operating Cash Inflows after Tax:** These are the expected returns to be generated from the use of the asset during its life.

The incremental operating cash flows can be computed using the following equation:

Incremental operating cash flow t = ΔCash revenues t – ΔCash Expenses t – ΔTaxes t = ΔNIt – ΔTaxes t

where Δ represents a change and ΔNIt is the change in net income associated with the project.

Calculation of Operating Cash Inflows

Operating Cash Inflows over a Project's Life

Profit after tax (PAT) + Depreciation *(Non-cash charges)* + Interest after tax *(Non-operating items)* = Annual cash inflows

CASH INFLOWS VERSUS PAT

Cash inflows are preferred over profits because cash flows are necessary to undertake the investment and meet operational expenses, not the accounting profit. Cash flows are based on the 'time value of money', not income. The computation of accounting income often includes non-cash items, such as depreciation and provisioning.

Therefore, 'operating cash inflows after taxes' are used in the calculation because that is the amount which represents the amount to be enjoyed by the shareholders.

(iii) **Terminal Cash Flows:** These are the cash flows that occur only at the end of the life of the asset. They denote the scrap value/salvage value of the asset.

CHECKLIST FOR CALCULATING CASH FLOWS:

- Consider incremental cash flows
- Focus on relevant cash flows
- Ignore sunk cost
- Ignore any other irrelevant cost.

Illustration 4.2: Calculation of incremental cash flows

A firm has an old fabrication plant with a remaining life of another three years. It is estimated to generate cash flows of Rs. 20,000, Rs. 10,000, and Rs. 5,000 during the next three years. Its book value is Rs. 50,000 and the market value is Rs. 20,000.

The firm is planning to replace it with the new machine for Rs. 70,000. The new machine is estimated to generate cash flows of Rs. 50,000, Rs. 45,000, and Rs. 35,000 for the next three years. Both old and new equipment have zero resale value after three years. Taxes are assumed to be zero.

What are the incremental cash flows that will occur if the old machine is replaced?

Solution

Cash Flows Computation (Rs.)

	0	*1*	*2*	*3*
Cash flows from new machine (1)	-70,000	50,000	45,000	35,000
Less: Cash flows from old machine (2)	+20,000	20,000	10,000	5,000
Incremental cash flows (1–2)	**-50,000**	**30,000**	**35,000**	**30,000**

Note: The book value of Rs. 50,000 of the old machine is not considered as it is not relevant here. It is 'sunk cost'.

Inference: After spending Rs. 50,000 of incremental cash outflows, the firm enjoys Rs. 95,000 of incremental cash inflows, ignoring the time value of money.

Illustration 4.3: Effect of tax implications

A company purchased a water cooler for its office staff a few years ago for Rs. 20,000. It wants to replace this with the new one in the market for Rs. 30,000. The company is subject to income tax at 25%. The present book value of the old asset is Rs. 5,000.

Calculate the net initial cash outflow if the company decides to replace the old water cooler, and it is sold for:

(a) Rs. 5,000
(b) Rs. 10,000
(c) Rs. 3,000

Solution

	Rs.
1. Cash outflow on the new asset	30,000
Less: Cash proceeds from the sale of old asset	5,000
Net cash outflow	**25,000**
2. Cash outflow on the new asset	30,000
Less: Cash proceeds from the sale of old asset	10,000
Add: Income tax liability on profit from the sale	20,000
of old asset (5,000 × 25 / 100)	1,250
Net cash outflow	**21,250**
3. Cash outflow on the new asset	30,000
Less: Cash proceeds from the sale of old asset	3,000
Less: Income tax saving on loss from the sale of	27,000
old asset (2,000 × 25 / 100)	500
Net cash outflow	**26,500**

References

1. Goel, Sandeep. 2015. *Capital Budgeting*. New York: Business Expert Press, p. 51.
2. Goel, Sandeep. 2015. *Capital Budgeting*. New York: Business Expert Press, p. 54.

5

CAPITAL BUDGETING EVALUATION TECHNIQUES

One of the most crucial responsibilities in capital budgeting is evaluation, since the outcome of an assessment determines the project's success. The project is evaluated using a variety of methods, including time-value analysis and others. The project's goals and nature, as well as the company's long-term growth and the optimisation of shareholders' wealth, are taken into consideration when choosing the capital investment appraisal techniques. The capital budgeting techniques are classified into the following two categories:

(a) Capital budgeting techniques not based on 'time value of money'
(b) Capital budgeting techniques based on 'time value of money'.

These techniques are categorised into the following two groups:

1. Non-discounted cash flow techniques
   (i) Payback period (PBP)
   (ii) Accounting rate of return (ARR)
2. Discounted cash flow (DCF) techniques
   (i) Discounted payback
   (ii) Net present value (NPV)
   (iii) Profitability index (PI)
   (iv) Internal rate of return (IRR)

DOI: 10.4324/9781003730163-7

Non-discounted Cash Flow Techniques

Payback Period

The 'payback period' is the conventional method used in capital budgeting decision. It is the simplest and the most widely used method for evaluating capital budgeting project.

It is defined as 'the time period required to recover the initial investment of the project'. The project with the shortest payback period is selected.

It is computed as:

$$\frac{\text{Initial investment}}{\text{Annual cash inflow}} \tag{5.1}$$

> **ACCEPTANCE/REJECTION RULE**
>
> If Payback period > predetermined period, reject the project and vice versa.

Illustration 5.1
Scenario 1: Even Cash Inflows

A project requires Rs. 40,000 as initial investment. The annual cash inflows generated are Rs. 5,000 for ten years. Calculate the payback period.

Solution

$$\text{Payback period} = \frac{\text{Initial inverstment}}{\text{Annual cash inflow}} \tag{5.2}$$

$$\frac{Rs.40,000}{Rs.5,000} = 8\,Years$$

Scenario 2: Uneven Cash Inflows

A project requires Rs. 25,000 as initial investment. The annual cash inflows for five years are Rs. 10,000, Rs. 9,000, Rs. 7,000, Rs. 4,000, and Rs. 2,000. Calculate the payback period.

Solution

Initial investment = Rs. 25,000

Year	*Cash inflows (Rs.)*	*Cumulative cash inflows (Rs.)*
1	10,000	10,000
2	9,000	19,000
3	7,000	26,000
4	4,000	30,000
5	2,000	32,000

In the years, Rs. 19,000 has been recovered. Rs. 6,000 is left to be recovered.

In the third year, the cash inflow is Rs. 7,000.

$$\begin{aligned}\text{So, the paback period} &= 2\,\text{years} + 6{,}000/7{,}000 \\ &= 2.85\,\text{years}\end{aligned} \tag{5.3}$$

Accounting Rate of Return (ARR)

The 'accounting (average) rate of return' (ARR) is the ratio of average net profit of the project to the assets employed for the project. It measures the rate of return on the project *using accounting profit* information. Therefore, it is closely related to ROI performance measure. The return from the project is compared with target ARR based on the firm's cost of capital for arriving at a decision.

It is computed as:

$$\frac{\textit{Average profit after tax}}{\textit{Averageinvestment / Original investment}} \times 100 \tag{5.4}$$

ACCEPTANCE/REJECTION RULE

If ARR > required rate of return, accept the project and vice versa.

Illustration 5.2: Aps Ltd is planning to invest in a project. The initial investment required for the project is Rs. 30,000. The expected earnings before interest, taxes, and depreciation (EBITDA) during the next three years is given below.

Year	*EBITDA for project (Rs.)*
1	12,000
2	15,000
3	18,000

The project is entirely funded by equity, so the interest is zero. Tax rate is 30%. Depreciation is charged on a straight-line basis. The scrap value is nil. Should the firm accept this project if the minimum accounting rate of return required by the company is 15%?

Solution

Years	*1*	*2*	*3*	*Average*
EBITDA	Rs. 12,000	15,000	18,000	**15,000**
Less: Depreciation	10,000	10,000	10,000	
EBIT	2,000	5,000	8,000	5,000
Less: Interest	–	–	–	
EBT	2,000	5,000	8,000	5,000
Less: Tax @ 30%	600	1,500	2,400	
PAT	1,400	3,500	5,600	3,500

$$\text{So, Accounting Rate of Return} = \frac{3{,}500}{30{,}000} \times 100 \qquad (5.5)$$

$$= 11.67\%$$

The company cannot accept this project, as its ARR is less than the minimum or standard rate of return.

Discounted Cash Flow (DCF) Techniques

Following steps are used in using the DCF methods:

(i) calculate the cash outflows and cash inflows,
(ii) discount the cash flows by 'discount factor', and
(iii) compare the discounted cash inflows with cash outflows to arrive at decision.

Discounted Payback Period

One of the major limitations of the payback method is that it does not consider the 'time value of money'. That's why 'discounted payback' is preferred over the payback method, as it overcomes this problem by discounting the cash flows and then calculating the payback period. It is a discounted version of the payback method.

Thus, *discounted payback period* is the time period taken in recovering the investment outlay on a present value basis. But it fails to consider the cash flows beyond the payback period.

***Illustration** 5.3*: A project requires an investment of Rs. 20,000. The cash flow generated by it for three years is as follows.

Years	*0*	*1*	*2*	*3*
Cash flows	(20,000)	12,000	8,000	5,000

The discounting factor is 8%. Calculate the payback and discounted payback.

Solution
The simple payback of the project is two years while discounted payback is 2.51 years, which is longer than simple payback because the discounted payback uses cash flows after discounting it with the cost of capital.

Years	*0*	*1*	*2*	*3*	*Simple payback*	*Discounted payback*
Cash flows	–20,000	12,000	8,000	5,000		
Cumulative cash flows		**12,000**	**20,000**	**25,000**	**2 years**	
PV factor @ 8%		0.926	0.857	0.794		
PV of cash flows		11,112	6,856	3,970		
Cumulative PV of cash flows		**11,112**	**17,968**	**21,938**		**2.51 years**

Net Present Value (NPV)

NPV is one of the most popular and widely used DCF methods. It discounts the future cash inflows and outflows using the target cost of capital. Simply, NPV is the difference between 'the present value of future cash inflows and the present value of cash outflows'. A positive value implies that the project is profitable and vice versa.

It is calculated as:

$$NPV = PV \text{ of cash inflows} - PV \text{ of cash outflows} \quad (5.6)$$

Mathematically, it is expressed as:

$$NPV = \left[\frac{C_1}{(1+k)} + \frac{C_2}{(1+k)^2} + \frac{C_3}{(1+k)^3} + \dots\dots + \frac{C_n}{(1+k)^n} \right] - C_0 \tag{5.7}$$

$$NPV = \sum_{t=1}^{n} \frac{C_t}{(1+k)^t} - C_0$$

Here, C_1, C_2 ... C_n represent future cash inflows
C_0 represents cash outflows
K is the discounting rate
t = time period

ACCEPTANCE/REJECTION RULE

If NPV > 0, accept the project and vice versa.

Illustration 5.4
Scenario 1: Annuity Cash Flows
A handloom project requires an initial investment of Rs. 10,000. It provides a net cash inflow of Rs. 5,000 each year for five years. If the cost of funds is 8%, calculate the net present value.

Solution
Net Present Value = PV of cash inflows – PV of cash outflows

PV factor of an annunity of Re 1 for 5 years at 8% per annum interest is Rs. 3.993

So, Present value of cash inflows = 5,000 × 3.993 = Rs. 19,965

Hence, NPV = 19,965 – 20,000 = –Rs. 35

The company should not undertake the project as the NPV is negative; in other words, the benefits associated with the investment are less than the costs associated with it.

Scenario 2: Mixed Stream Cash Flows

Enterprising Brothers Ltd is planning to buy software for manufacturing iPhones. The cost of the software is Rs. 60,000. Following are the cash flows associated with the project over its life period of five years.

Year	*Cash flows after tax*
1	Rs. 15,000
2	Rs. 20,000
3	Rs. 24,000
4	Rs. 22,500
5	Rs. 8,000

Determine whether the software should be invested in or not using NPV criteria, if the target return on capital is 9%.

Solution

Net present value = present value of inflows – present value of outflows

Present value of inflows =

$$\frac{15,000}{(1+0.09)}+\frac{20,000}{(1+0.09)^2}+\frac{24,000}{(1+0.09)^3}+\frac{22,500}{(1+0.09)^4}+\frac{8,000}{(1+0.09)^5} \quad (5.8)$$

Alternatively, using present value tables we get:

Year	*1*	*2*	*3*	*4*	*5*
PV at 9%	0.917	0.842	0.772	0.708	0.650

$$= 15,000 \times 0.917 + 20,000 \times 0.842$$

$$+24,000 \times 0.772 + 22,500 \times 0.708 + 8,000 \times 0.650$$

$$= 13,755 + 16,840 + 18,528 + 15,930 + 5,200 = \text{Rs.}70,253$$

$$\text{Hence, NPV} = 70,253 - 60,000 = \text{Rs. }10{,}253.$$

Present value of inflows

The company can purchase the software as the NPV is positive, in other words the benefits associated with the investment are greater than the costs associated with it.

Profitability Index (PI)/Benefit–Cost Ratio (B / C Ratio)

It is the ratio of 'present value of future cash inflows and the present value of cash outflows' at the required rate of return. The index is used instead of net present value in case of evaluating mutually exclusive proposals with different costs.

It is calculated as:

$$\text{PI} = \frac{\text{Present value of cash inflows}}{\text{Present value of cash outflows}} \tag{5.9}$$

ACCEPTANCE/REJECTION RULE

If PI > 1, accept the project and vice versa.

Example

Taking the example of Young Brothers Ltd in the above illustration of NPV,

PI will be:

$$\text{PI} = \frac{\text{Present value of cash inflows}}{\text{Present value of cash outflows}}$$

$$= Rs.\frac{70,253}{60,000} \tag{5.10}$$

$$= 1.17$$

Since the profitability index is more than one, the project can be invested in.

Internal Rate of Return (IRR)

It is the rate of return at which NPV is zero, i.e., the rate at which 'PV of cash inflows = PV of cash outflows'. It can also be called the break-even rate of discounted cash flows. This rate of return is then

compared with the budgeted rate of return to decide on the acceptance of the project.

Algebraically, it is expressed as:

$$C_0 = \frac{C_1}{(1+r)} + \frac{C_2}{(1+r)^2} + \frac{C_3}{(1+r)^3} + \ldots + \frac{C_n}{(1+r)^n}$$

$$C_0 = \sum_{t=1}^{n} \frac{C_t}{(1+r)^t} \tag{5.11}$$

$$= \sum_{t=1}^{n} \frac{C_t}{(1+r)^t} - C_0 = 0$$

Here, C_1, C_2 ... C_n represent future cash inflows

C_0 represents cash outflows

r is the rate of return to be calculated

t = time period

> **ACCEPTANCE/REJECTION RULE**
>
> If IRR > required rate of return, accept the project and vice versa.

Illustration 5.5: HAC Industries Ltd want to expand its business by investing either in Project A or in Project B. Both the projects involve an outlay of Rs. 10,000 and have a life span of three years. The cash flows after tax associated with Projects A and B are as follows:

Year	*Project A (Rs.)*	*Project B (Rs.)*
1	2,000	4,000
2	4,000	4,000
3	6,000	4,000

Based on the IRR criterion, determine which project the company should invest in?

Solution

IRR FOR PROJECT A

Let r represent the IRR of project A:

$$10,000 = \frac{2,000}{(1+r)} + \frac{4,000}{(1+r)^2} + \frac{6,000}{(1+r)^3}$$

$$\text{i.e.}\ 10,000 = 2,000 \times PVIF_{(r\%,1\,\text{year})} \tag{5.12}$$

$$+4,000 \times PVIF_{(r\%,2\,\text{years})} + 6,000 \times PVIF_{(r\%,3\,\text{years})}$$

The value of the right-hand side of the equation at 9% is Rs. 9,834.

The value of the right-hand side of the equation at 8% is Rs. 10,044.

Hence, r will lie between 8% and 9%. Interpolating these two values we get,

$$r = 8\% + (9\% - 8\%) \times \frac{(10,044 - 10,000)}{(10,044 - 9,834)} \tag{5.13}$$

$$= 8.21\%$$

IRR FOR PROJECT B

Let r represent the IRR of project B:

$$10{,}000 = \frac{4{,}000}{(1+r)} + \frac{4{,}000}{(1+r)^2} + \frac{4{,}000}{(1+r)^3} \tag{5.14}$$

The PVIFA at 9% is 2.531 and PVIFA at 10% is 2.487

NPV at 9% = 4,000 × 2.531 – 10,000 = 10,124 – 10,000 = 124

NPV at 10% = 4,000 × 2.487 – 10,000 = 9,948 – 10,000 = –52

Hence r will lie between these two values.

Interpolating the two values, we get:

$$r = 9\% + (10\% - 9\%) \times \frac{(10{,}124 - 10{,}000)}{(10{,}124 - 9{,}948)} = 9.70\% \tag{5.15}$$

Comment: IRR for Project Bis higher and hence, more profitable than Project A.

NPV VERSUS IRR

NPV is considered to be a better method for capital budgeting decision than IRR for the following reasons:

1. **Reinvestment of Cash Flows**: The NPV method assumes that the project's cash inflows are reinvested to earn the discounting rate, whereas the IRR assumes that the cash inflows are reinvested to earn the IRR. The NPV's assumption is more realistic in most situations because discounting rate is the financing cost whose recovery is the main criterion. IRR recovery is more of an interpolation.
2. **Multiple IRRs**: It is possible to have multiple IRRs for the same project. If the cash flows are non-conventional (e.g., positive cash flow in one year, negative cash flow in the next year), the IRR method will have more than one solution. The NPV method does not have this problem.

Case: Indian Herbal Products Ltd

Indian Herbal Products (IHP) is situated in the east. They want to expand in the west, and therefore wish to acquire an old plant l for Rs. 5,000 million. The additional equipment required for the project is Rs. 1,000 million. The plant has a time horizon of five years.

The corporate planning department of the company has done the profit forecasting for the mill's operation as given in the following table.

There is a survey cost of Rs. 5 million incurred in the first year of the project. Corporate office costs incurred is Rs. 200 million per annum and half is for the project. The plant's expected sale value is Rs. 3,200 million (Table 5.1).

Financing of the Project

The company proposes to finance the project:

(i) 100% by internal financing at cost of 9% and
(ii) No debt is used for the project.

TABLE 5.1 Profitability projections

	(Rs. in million)				
	Year				
	1	*2*	*3*	*4*	*5*
Sales	5,500	5,800	6,500	6,000	5,000
Materials and consumables	200	250	280	300	250
Wages and salaries	1,500	1,800	2,000	1,400	1,200
Selling and distribution costs	800	750	1,000	500	650
Depreciation (WDV @ 20%)	1,200	960	768	614	492
Corporate office costs	200	200	200	200	200
Profit (loss) before tax	1,600	1,840	2,252	2,986	2,208
Less: tax @ 30%	480	552	676	896	662
Profit after tax	1,120	1,288	1,576	2,090	1,546

Discussion Question

Should the project be accepted and financed? Advise using the suitable capital budgeting techniques.

Solution

Step 1: Calculate 'Initial Cash Outflows'

	(Rs. in million)
Cost of mill	5,000
Cost of equipment	1,000
Total capital investment/Total cash outlay	**6,000**

Step 2: Calculate 'Cash Inflows'

(a) Calculation of PAT

	(Rs. in million)					
	0	*1*	*2*	*3*	*4*	*5*
Sales		*5,500*	*5,800*	*6,500*	*6,000*	*5,000*
Less: Materials and consumables		200	250	280	300	250
Wages and salaries		1,500	1,800	2,000	1,400	1,200
Selling and distribution costs		800	750	1,000	500	650
Depreciation (WDV) @ 20%		1,200	960	768	614	492
Corporate office costs		100	100	100	100	100
Survey costs		5	–	–	–	–
Total expenses		3,805	3,860	4,148	2,914	2,692
Profit (loss) before tax		1,695	1,940	2,352	3,086	2,308
Less: tax @ 30%		509	582	706	926	692
Profit after tax		**1,187**	**1,358**	**1,646**	**2,160**	**1,616**

Notes: (1) Out of corporate office costs of Rs. 200 million, only half is incurred for the project. Thus, the 'Relevant cost' of Rs. 100 million is charged to the project above and (2) The cost of 9% is 'cost of capital*'.

(b) Calculation of Cash Inflows from PAT

To arrive at 'cash inflows', depreciation is added back to PAT.

	(Rs. in million)					
	0	1	2	3	4	5
Sales		5,500	5,800	6,500	6,000	5,000
Less: Materials and consumables		200	250	280	300	250
Wages and salaries		1,500	1,800	2,000	1,400	1,200
Selling and distribution costs		800	750	1,000	500	650
Depreciation (WDV) @ 20%		1,200	960	768	614	492
Corporate office costs		100	100	100	100	100
Survey costs		5	–	–	–	–
Total expenses		3,805	3,860	4,148	2,914	2,692
Profit (loss) before tax		1,695	1,940	2,352	3,086	2,308
Less: tax @ 30%		509	582	706	926	692
Profit after tax		1,187	1,358	1,646	2,160	1,616
Plus: depreciation		1,200	960	768	614	492
CFO		**2,387**	**2,318**	**2,414**	**2,774**	**2,108**

* For detailed discussion on 'cost of capital' refer to Chapter 7.

Step 3: Calculate NPV, IRR, and Payback

	(Rs. million)					
	0	*1*	*2*	*3*	*4*	*5*
Sales		5,500	5,800	6,500	6,000	5,000
Less: Materials and consumables		200	250	280	300	250
Wages and salaries		1,500	1,800	2,000	1,400	1,200

	(Rs. million)					
	0	1	2	3	4	5
Selling and distribution costs		800	750	1,000	500	650
Depreciation (WDV) @ 20%		1,200	960	768	614	492
Corporate office costs		100	100	100	100	100
Survey costs		5	–	–	–	–
Total expenses		3,805	3,860	4,148	2,914	2,692
Profit (loss) before tax		1,695	1,940	2,352	3,086	2,308
Less: tax @ 30%		509	582	706	926	693
Profit after tax		1,187	1,358	1,646	2,160	1,616
Plus: depreciation		1,200	960	768	614	492
CFO		**2,387**	**2,318**	**2,414**	**2,774**	**2,108**
Cash outlay	-6,000					
Salvage value						3,200
Book value (Cost – Accum. Dep.)						1,966
Profit on Sale						1,234
Tax loss on Profit (SV – BV)						-370
Net cash flows	-6,000	2,387	2,318	2,414	2,774	4,938
NPV at 9%	**5,180**					
IRR	**35%**					
Cumulative cash flows	6,000	2,387	4,705	7,119	9,893	14,831
Payback (years)				**2.54**		

Notes: (1) The 'last year cash inflows' consist of annual cash inflows, terminal cash flows and tax saving and (2) No debt employed here, therefore no interest cost.

Comment: In the above case, NPV is positive, that is Rs. 5,180 million and the IRR is higher than the discounting rate of 9%. So, it is advisable to purchase the plant.

The payback period is just 2.54 years.

WORKING

The computation of 'NPV' is discussed below:

1, 2, 3, 4, and 5

Discounting factor at 9% 0.917, 0.842, 0.772, 0.708, and 0.650

PV of cash inflows (Rs.) 2,188.88, 1,951.76, 1,863.61, 1,963.99, and 3,209.7

(*Net cash flows × discounting factor*)

NPV Cash inflows=Rs.111,77.29 million

PV cash outflows=Rs.6,000 million

NPV=RS.5,177.29 million

Similarly, IRR can be computed using the methodology as discussed earlier in the chapter.

EXCEL WAY

As discussed in Chapter 3, 'Time Value of Money', NPV and IRR can be used using Excel application of *fx* as under:

1. FORMULA: NPV (Rate, $Value_n$) – Cash outflows

Here, $Value_n$ = Cash $inflows_n$

2. FORMULA: IRR ($Values_n$)

Here, $Values_n$ = Cash outflow, Cash $inflow_n$

PART III

Investment Decision

B. Working Capital

6

WORKING CAPITAL MANAGEMENT

When it comes to financing business and economic development, the term *working capital* is extremely important. Working capital is defined as 'the firm's investment in short-term resources for running the business smoothly without any interruptions' from the standpoint of financing. Ensuring a company can sustain its operations, pay off short-term debt, and meet its daily expenses are the objectives of working capital management. Keeping an eye on current resources like cash, inventory, and accounts receivable and payable is part of managing working capital. Effective working capital management is essential to an organisation's long-term viability and expansion.

Meaning of Working Capital

In simple words, working capital means 'the capital used to carry out the day-to-day operations of a business'. This indicates whether a company has enough short-term assets to cover its short-term debt. Anything below 1 indicates negative working capital (W/C), while anything over 2 means that the company is not investing excess assets. Most scholars believe that a working capital ratio between 1.0 and 2.0 is sufficient.

The capital required for a business can be classified under two main categories:

- *Fixed capital*
- *Working capital*

DOI: 10.4324/9781003730163-9

Every business needs funds for two purposes: *for its establishment and to carry on its day-to-day operations.*

'Long-term funds' are required to create production facilities through the purchase of fixed assets, such as plant and machinery, land, building, furniture, and so forth. Investment in these assets represents that part of firm capital, which is invested on a permanent or fixed basis called *fixed capital.*

The funds are also needed for 'short-term purposes', that is for the purchase of raw material, payment of wages, and other day-to-day operations of business. These funds are known as *working capital.* In other words, working capital refers to that firm's capital, which is required for short-term assets or current assets. Funds thus invested in current assets keep revolving last and being constantly converted into cash and this cash flow is again converted into other current assets. Hence it is known as 'circulating or short-term capital'.

The working capital requirement of an organisation is dependent on its 'working capital cycle or operating cycle' as it is commonly referred to (Figure 6.1). The shorter the length of the cycle, the lower would be the working capital requirement and vice versa.

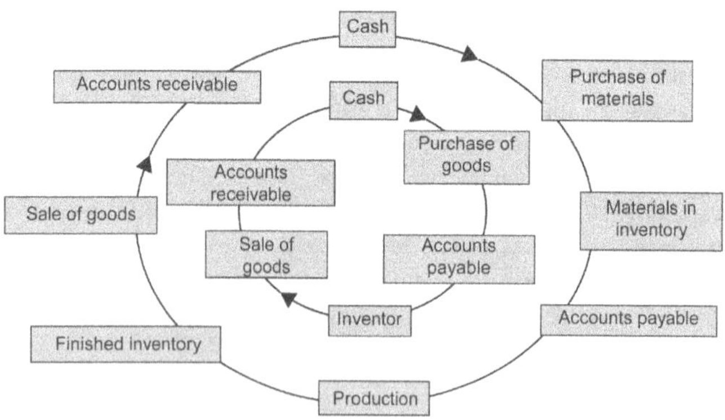

FIGURE 6.1 Operating cycle (working capital cycle)

OPERATING CYCLE AND CASH CYCLE

Operating cycle is the number of days taken by a company in realising its inventories in cash. It is the total of the time taken in selling inventories and the time taken in collecting cash from trade receivables. The length of the operating cycle determines the amount of investment required in working capital of an organisation. Operating cycle is a measure of the operating efficiency and working capital management of a company. A short operating cycle is good, as it indicates that the company's cash is not tied up for a longer period.

It is calculated as:

Operating cycle = Inventory conversion period + Debtors conversion period

Inventory conversion period is the average number of days taken by the company to sell its inventory. *Debtors' conversion period* is the time taken to realise receivables in cash.

Example: Assume 60 days are taken to deliver and process the raw material, and sell the finished goods to the customers. Customers take a further 40 days on average to pay.

Operating cycle = 60 inventory days + 40 debtor days = 100 days

Cash cycle (also called the cash conversion cycle) is another useful measure used to assess the operating efficiency of a company. It denotes the actual cash requirement to run the business operations.

Cash cycle = Operating cycle – Payment period to suppliers

Example: Taking the above example further, if the firm receives 30 days' credit from its suppliers.

Cash conversion cycle = 100 days – 30 creditor days = 70 days

Concept of Working Capital

Gross Working Capital

It refers to the firm's investment in 'total current assets' needed to operate over a normal business cycle. This implies the required investment in inventory, accounts receivable, cash, and other items listed as current assets on the firm's balance sheet.

Net Working Capital

Net working capital represents the difference between current assets and current liabilities. It may be positive or negative. Positive net working capital is that when current assets are more than current liabilities. But when current liabilities become more than current assets, then it is negative working capital. In this context, working capital financing concerns how a firm finances its current assets.

It is calculated as:

Working capital = Current assets – Current liabilities

How it works – example!

Following is the sample balance sheet of ABC Company.

	Amount (Rs.)		*Amount (Rs.)*
Cash	20,000	Accounts payable	10,000
Marketable securities	10,000	Bank overdraft	20,000
Accounts receivable	20,000	Accrued expenses	10,000
Inventory	30,000	Cash credit	20,000
Total current assets	80,000	**Total current liabilities**	60,000

FIGURE 6.2 Balance Sheet of ABC Company as of 31 March 2024

Using the working capital formula and the above information, we can see that ABC Company's working capital is:

Rs. 80,000 – Rs. 60,000 = Rs. 20,000

Constituents of Working Capital

Following are the components of working capital.

A. *Current Assets*

These assets are reasonably expected to be converted into cash within one year in the normal course of business. They include *cash and bank, accounts receivable, inventory, prepaid expenses,* and other liquid assets that can be readily converted to cash.

1. *Cash and Bank*

Cash is an asset that is in money form. It typically includes bank accounts and money market funds. Marketable securities, such as government securities/treasury bills, certificates of deposits are easily converted into cash within a short period of time and are thus called 'cash equivalents.'

2. *Accounts Receivable*

Accounts receivable (A/R) are amounts owed by customers for goods and services a company sold them on credit.

3. *Inventory*

Inventory includes raw materials, semi-finished goods, and finished goods lying unsold.

4. *Prepaid Expenses*

These assets arise on a balance sheet as a result of a business making payments for goods and services to be received in the near future. While prepaid expenses are initially recorded as assets, their value is expensed over time as the benefit is received onto the income statement, because unlike conventional expenses, the business will receive its benefit in the near future.

B. *Current Liabilities*

These are the company's debts or obligations that are due within one year. Current liabilities appear on the company's balance sheet and include *short-term debt, accounts payable, accrued liabilities,* and other debts.

1. *Short-term Debt*

Short-term debt includes any debt incurred by a company that is due within one year. The debt in this account is usually made up of short-term bank loans taken out by the company.

2. *Accounts Payable*

Accounts payable (A/P) are amounts owed to suppliers and other creditors for goods and services bought on credit.

3. *Accrued Liabilities*

Accrued liabilities are expenses that a business has incurred but has not yet been paid. A company can accrue liability for any number of items, like a pension account that will be used for paying the retirees in the future. Accrued liabilities are recorded as either short- or long-term liabilities on a company's balance sheet, depending upon the time period.

Estimation of Working Capital

The working capital requirement of an organisation is based on its 'operating cycle'. The different factors included here are *the conversion period in the production process, the holding period of inventory, the collection period to customers, the payment period from suppliers,* and so forth.

How working capital is computed is explained below with the help of the following illustration.

Illustration 6.1: Following are the details about the operating cycle of a typical manufacturing company.

Estimated production 3,00,000 units p.a.	
Cost breakup (per unit in Rs.)	Holding/process/collection period
Raw material 20	Raw material 2 months WIP
Labour 15	1/2 month finished goods
Manufacturing overheads 5	1 month debtors/receivables
Depreciation 5	1 month
Selling overheads 5	Creditors/payables 2 months
Total cost 50	Cash balance Rs. 5,00,000
Profit 10	
Selling price 60	

Calculate the monthly working capital requirement in the present case.

Solution

A. *Calculation of Requirement of Each Component of Working Capital*

	Rs.
1. Raw material	
Annual consumption (3,00,000 × Rs. 20)	60,00,000
monthly consumption	5,00,000
Average holding (5,00,000 × 2 months)	10,00,000
2. WIP	
Annual production cost (3,00,000 × Rs. (20 + 15 + 5)	120,00,000
Monthly production	10,00,000
Average holding (10,00,000 × 1/2 month)	5,00,000
3. Finished goods	
Annual production (3,00,000) × Rs. (20 + 15 + 5)	120,00,000

	Rs.
Monthly production	10,00,000
Average holding (10,00,000 × 1 month)	10,00,000
4. Debtors/receivables	
Annual cost of sales (3,00,000 × Rs. (20 + 15 + 5 + 5)	135,00,000
Monthly cost of sales	11,25,000
Average debtors (11,25,000 × 1 month)	11,25,000
5. Sundry creditors/payables	
Annual consumption (3,00,000 × Rs. 20)	60,00,000
Monthly consumption	5,00,000
Average creditors (5,00,000 × 2 months)	10,00,000

Note: Depreciation is not considered in the above computation, being a non-cash operating expenditure.

B. *Calculation of Net Working Capital*

I. Current assets	*Rs.*
Cash	5,00,000
Raw material	10,00,000
WIP	5,00,000
Finished goods	10,00,000
Debtors	11,25,000
Total	**41,25,000**
II. Current liabilities	10,00,000
Sundry creditors	
Net Working capital (I–II)	31,25,000

Types of Working Capital

The following are the different types of working capital required in an organisation:

Permanent Working Capital

As the operating cycle is a continuous process so the need for working capital also arises continuously. But the magnitude of

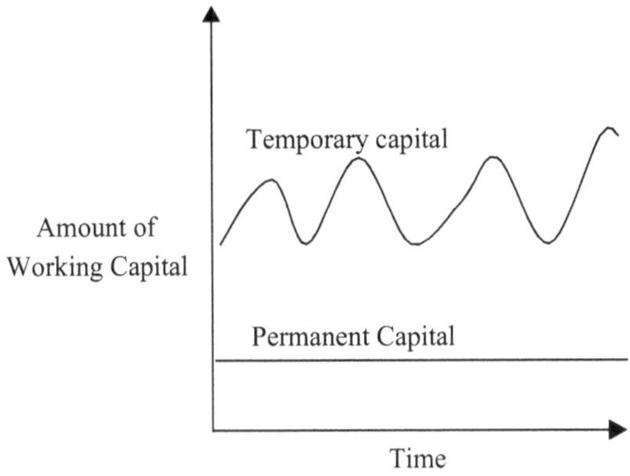

FIGURE 6.3 Types of working capital

current assets needed is not always the same; it increases and decreases over time. However, there is always a minimum level of current assets. This level is known as *'permanent or fixed working capital'*. It refers to the core current assets which are essential to run a business. Therefore, it is also called 'core working capital'.

Temporary Working Capital

The extra working capital needed to support the changing production and sales activities is called *'variable or temporary working capital'*.

These are shown in Figure 6.3.

Determinants of Working Capital

The working capital requirement depends upon various factors which are discussed below, though the importance of the influence of these determinants on working capital may differ from firm to firm.

1. *Nature and Size of Business*

The working capital of a firm basically depends upon the nature of its business; *for example*, public utility undertakings like electricity and water supply need less working capital because they offer deals in cash revenues, whereas trading and financial firms have very little investment in fixed assets but require a large sum of money invested in working capital.

The size of business also determines working capital requirement, and it may be measured in terms of scale of operations. The greater the size of operations, the larger the requirement of working capital.

2. *Manufacturing Cycle*

The manufacturing cycle also creates the need for working capital. The manufacturing cycle starts with the purchase and use of raw materials and completes with the production of finished goods. If the manufacturing cycle is longer, more working capital will be required and vice versa.

3. *Production Policy*

Production policy also determines the working capital level of a firm. If the firm has a steady production policy, it may require continuous working capital. But if the firms adopt a revolving production policy, which means to produce more during the lead demand season, then more working capital may be required at that time but not in other periods during the financial year. So, different production policies lead to a need for different types of working capital.

4. *Firm's Credit Policy*

The firm's credit policy directly affects the working capital requirement. If the firm has a liberal credit policy, the longer credit period will be provided to the debtors, so this will lead to more working capital requirements. With the liberal credit policy, the operating cycle length increases and vice versa.

5. *Sales Growth*

Working capital requirement is directly related to sales growth. If the sales are growing, more working capital will be needed due to the need for more raw materials, finished goods, and credit sales.

6. *Business Cycle*

Business cycle refers to alternate expansion and contraction in general business. In a boom period, a larger amount of working capital is required, whereas in a period of depression, a lesser amount of working capital is required.

Types of Working Capital Policy

The different types of working capital financing policy adopted by an organisation are explained below.

1. *Aggressive Working Capital Policy*

This is a 'high risk, high return policy'. It involves keeping a low amount of current assets by the enterprise. It finances the current assets through short-term sources. Therefore, it is risky and results in 'negative working capital'.

Here, the strategy is to defer the payments to the suppliers the maximum possible extent and to collect from the customers sooner. So, a business uses very little of its own cash, paying the creditors as late as it possibly can. It is a high-risk arrangement because if your creditors ask for their payments and, for some reason, you don't have enough money to pay them off, you might land up in trouble.

"MORE RISKY, LESS COSTLY"

Negative Working Capital: The Rationale!

Negative working capital occurs when current liabilities exceed current assets, which can lead to bankruptcy. In another scenario, negative working capital is a sign of managerial efficiency in a business with low inventory and accounts receivable (which means they operate on an almost strictly cash basis).

Negative Working Capital: Good or Bad?

'Ordinarily, having negative anything is not a good thing, but with operating working capital, it can be'.

Negative working capital is good if the following conditions are satisfied:

1. If payment of all short-term liabilities is on time.
2. With good sales and profit margins.
3. With proper inventory management.

If the above conditions are fulfilled, the working capital is funded by cash profits generated from the normal operating cycle and there is no strain on payment.

2. *Conservative Working Capital Policy*

This is the opposite of the aggressive approach. In this policy, you finance your current assets by long-term sources and keep a safety net for future uncertainty. This results in 'positive working capital'. So, this is the policy with the lowest risk, but it is less profitable as it reduces the money used in increasing the production.

"Less risky, more costly"

3. *Matching Working Capital Policy*

This policy is an arrangement where the current assets of the business are used perfectly to match the current liabilities. It is a medium-risk proposition. *For example*, if the creditor is due to be paid in five months, the company will ensure that there is enough cash to pay the creditor five months hence. It is also called a 'hedging approach'.

The following table (Table 6.1) *lists the working capital policy of the top ten Sensex companies. There is a mix of companies with positive and negative working capital, as discussed above. It verifies that the working capital policy of a company is not sector/industry specific.*

Working Capital Management: The Concept

Working capital management involves the relationship between a firm's short-term assets and its short-term liabilities. The management of working capital is concerned with the problems that arise in attempting to manage the current assets, current liabilities, and the inter-relationship that exists between them.

The basic goal of working capital management is to manage current assets and current liabilities of a firm in such a way that a satisfactory 'optimum level of working capital' is maintained; that is it is neither inadequate nor excessive. This is so because both inadequate and excessive working capital positions are bad for business.

Effective working capital management encompasses several aspects of short-term finance:

(i) *Maintaining adequate levels of cash.*
(ii) *Converting short-term assets (i.e., accounts receivable and inventory) into cash.*
(iii) *Controlling outgoing payments to vendors, employees, and others.*

To do this successfully, companies invest short-term funds in working capital portfolios of short-dated, highly liquid securities, or they maintain credit reserves in the form of bank lines

TABLE 6.1 Working capital policy of top ten companies by market capitalisation as on 13 September 2023

Company	*Industry*	*Market Capitalisation (Rs. in crores)*	*Working Capital (Rs. in crores)*
Reliance Industries Ltd	Refineries & Marketing	1659438.11	28,656.00
Tata Consultancy Services Ltd	Computers – Software & Consulting	1304653.06	53,460.00
HDFC Bank Ltd	Private Sector Bank	1245011.07	–
ICICI Bank Ltd	Private Sector Bank	692962.47	–
Infosys Ltd	Computers – Software & Consulting	621287.82	24,640.00
Hindustan Unilever Ltd	Diversified FMCG	588913.30	4,410.00
ITC Ltd	Diversified FMCG	565338.21	22,787.82
State Bank of India	Public Sector Bank	532308.48	–
Bharti Airtel Ltd	Telecom – Cellular & Fixed line services	511671.40	-37,668.00
Bajaj Finance Ltd	Non-Banking Financial Company (NBFC)	452954.78	-1,987.09

Sources: List of companies is taken from: https://www.bseindia.com/markets/equity/EQReports/TopMarketCapitalization.aspx.

Working capital figure is taken from 'Ace Analyser' database (https://www-aceanalyser-com) and is as on March, 2023.

Note: Rs. 1 crore = Rs. 10 million.

of credit or access to financing by issuing commercial paper or other money market instruments.

> The scope of working capital management includes areas of 'transactions', 'analysis', and 'focus' of current resources:
>
> (i) *Transactions* include payments for trade, financing, and investment relations with financial institutions and trading partners that must be maintained to ensure that the transactions work effectively.
> (ii) *Analysis* of working capital management activities is required so that appropriate strategies can be formulated and implemented.
> (iii) *Focus* requires that organisations of all sizes today must have a global viewpoint with a strong emphasis on liquidity.

Effective execution requires managing and coordinating several tasks within the company, including managing short-term investments, granting credit to customers and collecting on this credit, managing inventory, and managing payables. It also requires reliable cash forecasts, as well as current and accurate information on transactions and bank balances.

Equally important is to note that working capital needs vary from industry to industry, especially considering how different industries depend on expensive equipment.

Significance of Working Capital Management

Working capital is the lifeblood of business. It is very essential to maintain the smooth running of a business. No business can run successfully without an adequate amount of working capital. The main advantages or importance of working capital are as follows:

1. *Sound Liquidity*

Working capital is a common measure of a company's efficiency, liquidity, and overall health. Positive working capital indicates that the company is able to pay off its short-term liabilities immediately, whereas negative working capital indicates that a company is unable to do so. This is why any decrease in working capital suggests that a company is becoming overleveraged and struggling to sustain. Therefore, efficient working capital management is of crucial importance for maintaining sound liquidity in the current state of business.

2. *Smooth Business Operations*

Working capital helps to operate the business smoothly without any financial problem for making the payment of short-term liabilities. Purchase of raw materials and payment of salary, wages, and overheads can be made without any delay. Any day-to-day financial requirement can be met without any shortage of funds and interrupting the flow of production.

3. *Increase in Goodwill*

Sufficient working capital enables a business concern to make prompt payments and hence helps in creating and maintaining goodwill. Goodwill is enhanced because all current liabilities and operating expenses are paid in time.

4. *Ease of Obtaining Loan*

A firm having adequate working capital, high solvency, and a good credit rating can arrange loans from banks and financial institutions on easy and favourable terms.

5. *Risk Management*

Adequate working capital enables a firm to face business crises in emergencies such as depression. A working capital shortage can cause a business to fail even though it may actually turn out to have a profit. Therefore, the timing of payment, collection policies, and asset purchases play an important role in mitigating the risk of business shut-down.

Working Capital Analysis of Nestle India and Dabur India

The working capital practices of leading fast-moving consumer goods (FMCG) sector companies in India, *Nestle India Ltd* and *Dabur India Ltd* are discussed here on a comparative basis. *They operate globally; therefore, their analysis will be relevant for all.* This will also provide an insight into *the trend of positive and negative working capital and its 'impact on profitability'. The data has been taken from the annual reports of the companies.*

Indian FMCG Sector

Fast-moving consumer goods (FMCG) sector is India's fourth-largest sector and has been expanding at a healthy rate over the years because of rising disposable income, a rising youth population, and rising brand awareness among consumers. With household and personal care accounting for 50% of FMCG sales in India, the industry is an important contributor to India's GDP. India is a country that no FMCG player can afford to ignore due to its middle-class population, which is larger than the total population of the USA. The Indian FMCG market continues to rise as more people start to move up the economic ladder and the benefits of economic progress become accessible to the public.[1]

Nestle and Dabur's analysis of working capital practices is discussed below .

Comment: Nestle is with negative WC and Dabur is with positive WC. In this case, Nestle with negative working capital has higher sales and is more profitable than Dabur with positive working capital. On comparing the current ratio of both the companies, we find that the current ratio of Nestle is much below 1, implying that it is riskier for the creditors as compared to Dabur, whose current ratio is approximately around 1. But

TABLE 6.2 Indian FMCG – working capital position

Nestle India (negative working capital)	*December 2008*	*December 2009*	*December 2010*	*December 2011*
Net current assets (Rs. in crores)	**–423**	**–598**	**–657**	**–884**
Net sales (Rs. in crores)	**4,329**	**5,142**	**6,260**	**7,491**
Profit before depreciation and tax (PBDT)%	20%	20%	20%	21%
Current ratio (in times)	0.66	0.60	0.62	0.42
Quick ratio (in times)	0.29	0.24	0.27	0.24
Inventory turnover ratio (in times)	11.39	11.61	12.33	11.60
Debtors turnover ratio (in times)	87.37	93.68	98.22	83.83
Average raw materials Holding Period (days)	25	31	22	30
Average finished goods Holding Period (days)	26	22	23	22
Number of days in working capital	**–35**	**–42**	**–38**	**–42**

Note: Rs. 1 crore = Rs. 10 million.

Dabur India (Positive Working Capital)

	March 2008	*March 2009*	*March 2010*	*March 2011*
Net current assets (Rs. in crores)	**–34**	**276**	**30**	**243**
Net sales (Rs. in crores)	**2,094**	**2,408**	**2,867**	**3,274**
Profit before depreciation and tax (PBDT)%	19%	19%	20%	20%
Current ratio (in times)	0.91	1.19	0.93	0.99
Quick ratio (in times)	0.58	0.99	0.68	0.78
Inventory turnover ratio (in times)	12.52	10.94	11.31	8.65
Debtors turnover ratio (in times)	25.94	22.63	23.62	19.67
Average raw materials Holding Period (days)	46	45	53	63
Average finished goods holding period (days)	20	21	22	29
Number of days in working capital	**–6**	**41**	**4**	**27**

Note: Rs. 1 crore = Rs. 10 million.

this negative working capital is leveraged by Nestle to its advantage and contributing to higher return generation.

Reference

1. IBEF. 2023. *FMCG Industry in India*, https://www.ibef.org/industry/fmcg (accessed on 26 August 2023).

PART IV

Financing Decision

7

COST OF CAPITAL

After choosing a project, the next crucial step is to finance it. The project's success or failure may be determined by the discount rate chosen during the capital budgeting process. *Equity* and *debt** are the most popular forms of funding that are utilised to fund projects. Depending on how well they balance risk and return, these financing options are employed. The type of financing used for the project determines the discount rate.

What is Cost of Capital?

It is 'the cost of acquiring funds for investment in a project'. It is also referred to as *discount rate, cut-off rate, hurdle rate,* or *target rate of return*. In this context, 'total cost of capital' and 'weighted average cost of capital' (WACC) are used interchangeably.

The computation of cost of capital is important on account of the following reasons:

1. **Capital Investment Decision:** The cost of capital is used as a yardstick by the management to decide on the selection of a project.
2. **Capital Structure Decision:** The cost of various sources of finance is used as the factor for selecting the optimum mix of funds for financing the project.

DOI: 10.4324/9781003730163-11

Classification of Costs

The costs of sources of finance can be classified into the following two categories:

1. **Explicit Costs:** These are the fixed costs that are paid by the firm to procure a source of finance. They consist of:
   (a) *Debt*
   (b) *Preference shares.*
2. **Implicit Costs:** These costs are not fixed and assured like explicit costs. They are an opportunity cost. They consist of:
   (a) *Equity shares*
   (b) *Retained earnings.*

Computation of Cost of Capital

The process of computation of cost of capital comprises the following steps:

1. Compute 'Specific Costs'.
   (i) *Cost of debt*
   (ii) *Cost of preference shares*
   (iii) *Cost of equity*
   (iv) *Cost of retained earnings.*
2. Assign 'Weights to Specific Costs'.
   (i) Book value weights versus market value weights
3. Multiply (1) by (2) to get the 'cost of capital' (WACC).

$ko = kdwd + kpwp + kewe + krwr$

Computation of Specific Costs

1. Cost of Debt

The debt or loan component has an explicit cost as mentioned above. The cost of debt provides a tax benefit to the company for interest payments, i.e., interest paid by the company on debt is tax deductible. *(See the example below.)*

TAX SHIELD ON INTEREST EXAMPLE

30% tax rate

Co. A (Zero debt) Co. B (Rs. 3,000 debt @ 10%)

EBIT	*5,000*	*5,000*
Less: Interest EBT		300
Less: Tax PAT	5,000	4,700
Effective interest rate	1,500	1,410
PAT	3,500	3,290

Effective rate = I (1 – t) = 10 (1 – 0.30) = 7%

So, tax reduces the effective rate of debt for the company.

It is calculated as follows:

$$\text{Cost of debt}\left(kd\right) = \frac{\text{I}}{\text{NP}}\left(1 - \text{t}\right) \tag{7.1}$$

Here, I = Annual interest payment

NP = Sale proceeds of debentures (par value – discount + premium – floatation cost)

t = Tax rate

***Illustration** 7.1*: A company issues 10% perpetual debentures of Rs. 2 million at a face value of Rs. 1,000.

The company is in 30% tax bracket. Calculate the cost of debt (after tax) if the debentures are issued at (1) par, (2) 10% discount, and (3) 10% premium.

Solution

(1) Issued at par

$$kd = \frac{I}{NP}(1-t) = \frac{100}{1,000}(1-0.30) = 0.07(7\%) \tag{7.2}$$

(2) Issued at discount

$$kd = \frac{I}{NP}(1-t) = \frac{100}{900}(1-0.30) = 0.077(7.7\%) \tag{7.3}$$

(3) Issued at premium

$$kd = \frac{I}{NP}(1-t) = \frac{100}{1,000}(1-0.30) = 0.063(6.3\%) \tag{7.4}$$

2. Cost of Preference Capital

Like debt capital, preference shares also have an explicit cost as the rate of dividend on preference shares is fixed and known. But the dividend paid to preference shareholders is not tax deductible, so there is no tax benefit to the company.

It is calculated as follows:

$$\text{Cost off preference share}(\text{kp}) = \frac{D}{NP} \tag{7.5}$$

Hera, D = Preference dividend

NP = Sale proceeds of preference shares (par value – discount + premium – floatation cost)

***Illustration** 7.2*: A company raises preference share capital for perpetuity of 1 million by issue of 10% preference shares of Rs. 100 each. The company is in 30% tax bracket. Calculate the cost of preference capital when they are issued at (1) par, (2) 10% discount, and (3) 10% premium.

Solution

(1) Issued at par

$$kp = \frac{D}{NP} = \frac{10}{100} = 0.1(10\%) \tag{7.6}$$

(2) Issued at discount

$$kp = \frac{D}{NP} = \frac{10}{90} = 0.11(11\%) \tag{7.7}$$

(3) Issued at premium

$$kp = \frac{D}{NP} = \frac{10}{110} = 0.090(9.0\%) \tag{7.8}$$

3. Cost of Equity Capital

It is an imputed cost as there is no fixed rate of return paid to equity shareholders. The dividend paid to equity shareholders is variable. In addition, the return to equity shareholders also consists of market returns. Thus, the cost of equity capital (COEC) is the rate of return that the firm must earn to meet equity shareholders' expectations for maximising their wealth. It is commonly calculated by the *Capital Asset Pricing Model (CAPM).*

CAPITAL ASSET PRICING MODEL (CAPM)[1]

The CAPM is the most widely used method to calculate 'cost of equity'. It describes 'risk-return' trade-off for securities, implying thereby 'the higher the risk involved of a stock, the higher will be the return expected by shareholders'. It is based on the following assumptions:

(i) *Efficiency of security markets*
(ii) *Investors' preferences for an optimum mix of risk-return.*

CAPM classifies the 'investment risk' into two categories:

1. *Diversifiable/Unsystematic risk:* Risk that can be reduced and controlled.
   (e.g. compensation policy of the company, strikes, and lockouts)
2. *Non-diversifiable/Systematic risk/Market risk:* Risk which is uncontrollable.
   (e.g. interest rate changes, inflation)

The investors are sensitive to the 'systematic risk'. So, the measurement of non-diversifiable/systematic risk is relevant for investment decision-making. The measurement of non-diversifiable risk/systematic risk of an investment/security is measured by the 'beta' coefficient.

CAMP Equation: $ke = Rf + b(km - Rf)$

Here,

ke = cost of equity capital

Rf = the risk-free rate of return

km = expected market return, i.e., return expected on the market portfolio of shares

$km - Rf$ = risk premium (difference between the expected market return and risk-free rate of return)

b = beta of the firm's share (systematic risk of an equity share in relation to the market)

Here,

Beta Coefficient and Its Application!

'"Beta" (β) is a measure of the volatility or sensitivity of a security's return in relation to changes in the return of the stock market'.

Categories of Beta

(i) **Aggressive Beta:** Shares with beta greater than 1 are considered aggressive beta stocks. They are relatively riskier than other stocks.

Example: Beta for State Bank of India (SBI) for July 2014 to June 2015 was 1.28. In the same sector (banking sector), the Beta of Axis Bank Ltd was higher than SBI at 1.83.[2]

This shows greater volatility, being aggressive beta stocks. Further, this proves that there can be two stocks in the same sector in the same 'risk zone' but with different degrees of risk.

(ii) **Neutral Beta:** Shares with beta equal to 1 are considered average beta stocks.

(iii) **Conservative/defensive Beta:** Shares with beta less than 1 are considered defensive beta stocks. They are less risky than other stocks.

Example: Beta of Maruti Suzuki India Ltd (MSIL) for July 2014 to June 2015 was 0.81, which indicates lower volatility. But in the same sector (automobile sector), Beta for Tata Motors Ltd was 1.41, indicating greater volatility than Maruti.[3]

This shows that there can be two stocks in the same sector but in different 'risk zones', unlike in the above example. As Maruti is a defensive beta stock, whereas Tata Motors is an aggressive beta stock.

Calculation of Beta

$$\beta_j = \frac{\text{Covariance}\, im}{\text{Variance}\, m}$$

$$= \text{Co-movements of individual stock and market Index volatility}$$

$$\beta_j = \frac{\text{Covar}_{j,m}}{\sigma_m^2} \tag{7.9}$$

$$= \frac{\sigma_j \sigma_m \text{Cor}_{j,m}}{\sigma_m \times \sigma_m} = \frac{\sigma_j}{\sigma_m} \times \text{Cor}_{j,m}$$

Illustration 7.3: The financial manager of New Ventures applies the CAPM to determine the firm's cost of equity capital. The financial analyst of the firm provides the following information about the equity funds:

Risk-free rate is currently 7%. Market return is 11%.
Firm's beta is 1.4.

Solution

$$\begin{aligned} ke &= Rf + \beta(Km - Rf) \\ &= 7\% + 1.4(11\% - 7\%) \\ &= 7\% + 1.4(4\%) \\ &= 12.6\% \end{aligned} \tag{7.10}$$

4. Cost of Retained Earnings

Like equity, retained earnings (reserves and surplus) also have an implicit cost as they do not involve any explicit payments by the management.

Cost of retained earnings is the return sacrificed by the equity shareholders. In other words, the cost of retained earnings is *the opportunity cost* of retained earnings which is equal to the cost of equity as follows:

So $kr = ke$

Assigning Weights to Specific Costs

At this stage, the proportion of each source of fund is determined in the total capital structure of the company.

The weights assigned may be either:

(a) *Historical weights*

These weights are assigned with the current capital structure as the basis. The weights here can again be:

(i) *book value weights*
(ii) *market value weights*

Market value weights are usually preferred over book value weights for assigning weights in calculating WACC.

(b) *Marginal weights*

These weights are assigned in the ratio of new capital to be raised.

So the weights here are for the new capital structure(s).

Multiplication of Specific Costs with Weights to Get Total Cost

This is the last stage of computing total cost of capital. The costs arrived at stage (1) are multiplied with the respective weights in stage (2) to arrive at 'WACC'.

Weighted Average Cost of Capital (WACC)

$ko = \Sigma\, wiki$

$ko = kd\,(1 - t)wd + kewe + kpwp$

Here, ko = WACC

wd, we, wp = weights of each fund in the total capital structure

***Illustration** 7.4*: Ambitions Ltd is a one-year-old company. Following is its capital structure for 2023. Calculate the total cost of capital of the firm for business valuation, using (a) book value weights and (b) market value weights:

Source	*Book value (Rs.)*	*Market value (Rs.)*
Equity Share Capital (Rs. 10 shares)	30,000	40,000
Preference Share Capital	10,000	10,000
Debentures	10,000	11,000

The after-tax cost of different sources of finance is as follows:
Equity Share Capital: 14%; Preference Share Capital: 9%; Debentures: 7%.

Solution

(a) *WACC (Book Value Weights)*

Source (1)	*Amount (Rs.) (2)*	*Proportion/ weight (3)*	*After tax cost (4)*	*Weighted cost (3) × (4)*
Equity Share Capital	30,000	0.6	14%	8.4%
Preference Share Capital	10,000	0.2	9%	1.8%
Debentures	10,000	0.2	7%	1.4%
	50,000			**11.6%**

Here, Weighted Average Cost of Capital (*ko*) = **11.6%**

(b) *WACC (Market Value Weights)*

Source (1)	*Amount (Rs.) (2)*	*Proportion/ weight (3)*	*After tax cost (4)*	*Weighted cost (3) × (4)*
Equity Share Capital	40,000	0.655	14%	9.17%
Preference Share Capital	10,000	0.16	9%	1.44%
Debentures	11,000	0.18	7%	1.26%
	61,000			**11.87%**

Here, Weighted Average Cost of Capital (*ko*) = **11.87%**

Comment: WACC according to market value weights is higher than the WACC as per book value weights.

Note

* Sources of finance are discussed in detail in Chapter 8.

References

1. Goel, Sandeep. 2015. *Capital Budgeting*. New York: Business Expert Press, p. 122.
2. BSE. www.bseindia.com/indices/betavalues.aspx (accessed on 5 June 2017).
3. BSE, www.bseindia.com/indices/betavalues.aspx (accessed on 5 June 2017).

8

CAPITAL STRUCTURE PLANNING

After computing the cost of capital, the firm determines its 'capital structure' as a part of the financing decision. When choosing a capital structure, the weighted average cost of capital, or WACC, is useful. It serves as the foundation for assessing different funding sources, assisting the business in determining whether or not to obtain the necessary funding source. By using a suitable capital mix, every company seeks to minimise its weighted average cost of capital (WACC), since a lower WACC enables a company to distribute higher profits to its owners. To maximise shareholder wealth, a company wants to have the ideal capital mix of debt and equity.

The 'financing decision' of a firm includes a consideration of three principal responsibilities of the finance manager. These are:

(a) Estimation of total financial requirements of the business enterprise;
(b) Identification of sources of finance and determining the financing mix; and
(c) Exploring sources of finance and raising the required finance.

> The 'financing decision' of a project or enterprise covers two inter-related aspects:

DOI: 10.4324/9781003730163-12

(a) Determination of an appropriate 'financial/capital structure'.
(b) Raising the required amount of funds.

Capital Structure Meaning

The resources' requirement of a firm can be financed either by owners' equity or borrowed funds. The owners' funds comprise ordinary shares or retained earnings; the borrowed funds denote loans from banks and financial institutions and public.

The various means of financing represent the financial structure of an enterprise. The 'liability plus equity' side of the balance sheet represents the *financial structure* of a company.

FINANCIAL STRUCTURE VERSUS CAPITAL STRUCTURE

The 'financial structure' refers to the *total amount of funds* of an enterprise. Traditionally, short-term borrowings are excluded from the list of methods of financing the firm's capital expenditure, and therefore, the *long-term claims* are said to form the 'capital structure' of an enterprise.

Capital structure is the composition of debt and equity. Determination of an optimal capital structure is a significant managerial decision. It influences the shareholder's return and risk. Consequently, the market value of the shares may be affected by the capital structure decision.

Types of Business Finance

Finance used in business is of the following kinds.

1. *Long-term Finance*

Long-term finance refers to that category of funds whose repayment is generally more than a ten-year period. It is raised from shareholders, debenture holders, financial institutions, and retained earnings.

Such type of finance is used for investment in fixed assets, such as land, buildings, plants, machinery, furniture, fixtures, and so forth. Long-term finance is used for meeting the permanent needs of business. Such finance cannot be taken out of the business without closing down the firm or without reducing the scale of operations.

2. *Medium-term Finance*

Medium-term/intermediate-term finance is that category of finance whose repayment can be projected within a planning cycle of reasonable length of time. It is raised for a period of more than one year but less than ten years from debenture holders, financial institutions, public deposits, and commercial banks. This type of finance is required for investment in permanent working capital and for repayment of assets.

3. *Short-term Finance*

Short-term finance is that category of finance which is employed by an enterprise for day-to-day operations. It is used for meeting obligations of a time period of a year or less. It is raised from trade credit and commercial banks and is represented by current liabilities and provisions. It is invested in current assets which are also known as 'working capital'.

Instruments of Finance

A business firm can raise funds from two main sources: owned funds and borrowed funds.

Owned funds refer to the funds provided by the owners. In a *proprietorship*, the proprietor himself provides the owned funds from his personal resources. In a *partnership firm*, the ownership funds are contributed by the partners jointly. In a *joint stock company*, owned funds are raised through the issue of shares and reinvestment of earnings.

Borrowed funds refer to the borrowings of a business firm. In a company, borrowed funds consist of the funds raised from debenture holders, financial institutions, public deposits, and commercial banks. Thus, the various instruments of finance may be divided as shown in Figure 8.1.

1. *Shares*

The issue of shares is the most important source of raising long-term finance. The 'share' indicates the interest of a shareholder in the assets and profits of a company. Shares can be issued in the following forms:

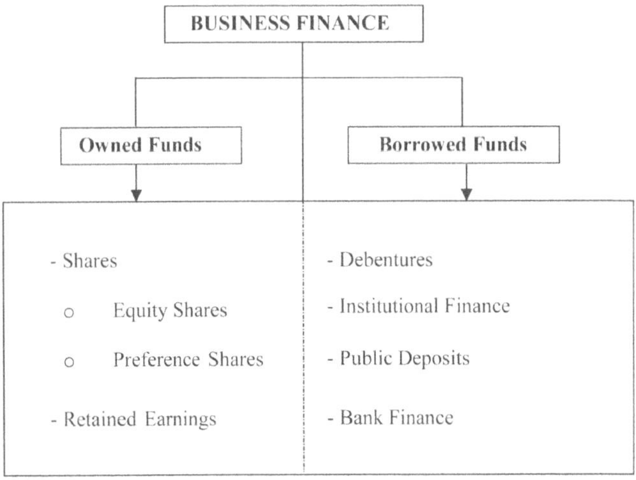

FIGURE 8.1 Instruments of finance

(a) *Equity (ordinary) Shares*

Equity shares are real owners of a company as they are paid last after everyone has been paid out of profits of the company. They do not carry any special or preferential rights in the payment of annual dividend or repayment of capital.

(b) *Preference Shares*

Preference shares are those shares which carry certain special or preferential rights in the payment of dividend and repayment of capital as compared to equity shareholders.

2. *Retained Earnings*

Retained earnings, also referred to as 'reserves and surplus', are the profits which have not been distributed as dividends but have been kept for reinvestment in business.

3. *Debentures*

Debentures represent the borrowings of a company for a fixed rate of interest to be paid to the debenture holders and repayment to them before anything is paid to other fund providers.

4. *Institutional Finance*

Institutional finance consists of financing from the central and state level financial institutions to the business firms, for example, *IFCI Ltd* and state finance corporations *(SFCs)*.

5. *Public Deposits*

Public deposits refer to the deposits received by a company from the public as loan or debt.

6. *Bank Finance*

Bank finance refers to the finance raised from commercial banks. Commercial banks are an important source of short-term and medium-term finance for the business.

Factors Affecting Capital Structure

There are various factors which govern the capital structure decision. They should be duly considered before taking any rational decision regarding capital structure. They are as follows.

1. *Profitability*

It is logically the first step in the direction of designing a firm's capital structure. The profitability status of the company affects the choice between debt and equity for capital mix. This analysis is based on the 'Earnings before Interest and Tax – Earnings per Share (EBIT – EPS)' relationship as EBIT should be higher than the interest payment on debt funding for stability of the company. EPS is a measure of a firm's performance; therefore, the EBIT/EPS analysis information is extremely useful to the finance manager in arriving at an appropriate financing decision.

2. *Liquidity*

The analysis of the liquidity of the firm is an important factor in capital structure planning in addition to profitability analysis. It is significant in the context of the risk of insolvency as interest payments on debt capital affect the cash flows of the company.

3. *Cost of Raising Capital*

The cost of raising finance has an important influence on the capital mix. The cost of equity share capital is higher than that of debenture and preference share capital. Debentures are a cheaper source of finance because the interest payable on debentures entitles the tax benefit to the company.

4. *Stability of Enterprise*

The nature of stability of the enterprise is one of the important factors affecting the capital structure of an enterprise. Business concerns with stable earning may raise funds by issues of debentures or preference shares because they will not feel the burden of fixed cost. On the other hand, the companies with fluctuating earnings rely more on equity share capital for raising their funds.

5. *Control*

The control factor also determines the type of capital to be raised. If the management is not prepared for the dilution of control, it will prefer to raise capital through borrowings, as the lenders cannot participate in the management of the company. If the management is prepared, it may go for the equity capital.

6. *Flexibility of Financial Structure*

Flexibility means the firm's ability to change its capital structure to the needs of the changing conditions. A capital structure is flexible if it is possible to acquire additional capital either through owned capital or through borrowed capital. So, if a company wants greater flexibility, it must have enough scope for addition to capital either through owned capital or borrowed capital.

7. *Capital Market Conditions*

Capital market conditions also affect the availability of a particular type of capital. In the case of a boom, people will like to invest in shares as they expect increasing profits; during a depression, they will like to invest in debentures so that they do get a given return on their investment.

8. *Legal Requirements*

The state regulations regarding the issue of securities also have a bearing on the capital structure of a company. This is particularly true in the case of Indian banking companies which have to abide by the provisions of the Banking Regulation Act, 1949 for issuing the securities.

Concept of Leverage

Leverage refers to any method or technique followed by a firm to multiply its gains. In other words, it is the employment of an asset or source of funds for which the firm has to pay a fixed cost or return. It is used by the company to maximise shareholders' value.

> The leverage can be either 'operating' leverage or 'financial' leverage. The use of fixed operating costs by a firm to magnify EBIT is called *operating leverage.* The use of fixed financing costs by a firm to magnify EPS is termed as *financing leverage.*

Leverage Ratio

This ratio is used to calculate the amount of fixed obligations involved in a company's structure and its ability to meet those obligations. As mentioned above, the leverage ratios are of two types: operating leverage ratio and financial leverage ratio.

1. **Operating Leverage Ratio:** It is the degree of fixed operating costs involved in a project. So, a firm with lower sales is a highly leveraged firm and affirm with higher sales is a low leveraged firm. It is calculated as:

$$\text{DOL} = \frac{\text{Percentage change in EBIT}}{\text{Percentage change in sales}} \tag{8.1}$$

Here, DOL = Degree of operating leverage

The higher the degree of operating leverage, the greater the operating risk and vice versa.

2. **Financial Leverage Ratio:** It is the degree of long-term debt involved in the financial structure of a firm. It is also called the 'debt to equity ratio'. Its accepted norm is 2:1. A high financial leverage ratio indicates risk of payment of interest and repayment of principal. It is calculated as:

$$\text{DFL} = \frac{\text{Percentage change in EPS}}{\text{Percentage change in EBIT}} \tag{8.2}$$

DFL = Degree of financial leverage

The higher the degree of financial leverage, the higher the financial risk and vice versa.

FINANCIAL LEVERAGE* AND SHAREHOLDER'S WEALTH

The primary motive of a company in using 'financial leverage' is to magnify the shareholder's returns, given the fact that the fixed financial cost is lower than the firm's rate of return (ROI). So, the difference between the earnings generated by assets financed by the fixed charges funds and costs of these funds is distributed to the shareholders as wealth in the form of higher EPS.

*Financial leverage is also referred to as 'trading on equity'.

Measures of Leverage: The ratios which measure how financially sound a company is to meet its long-term obligations are known as 'leverage or solvency ratios'. There are three common solvency ratios:

- Debt–Equity Ratio = Debt / Equity
- Interest Coverage Ratio = EBIT / Interest on long-term loans
- Debt Service Coverage Ratio = CFO / Interest + Principal payments

Factors Determining Financial Leverage

The financial leverage is subject to the following factors:

1. **Adequate Return:** A company can have 'trading on equity' only when the rate of return on total capital employed is more than the rate of interest on debentures or dividend on preference shares.
2. **Stable Earnings:** Trading on equity is beneficial only for those companies which have stable earnings. The reason being is that both interest and preference dividend impose a recurring burden on the company. In the absence at stable profits, the company may face serious financial difficulties in case of trade depression.
3. **Security:** There must be sufficient fixed assets to offer as security to lenders for trading on equity.
4. **Risk Consideration:** Every rupee of extra borrowings increases the risk. This results in an increase in the expected rate of interest by the subsequent lenders. Thus, borrowings become costlier, ultimately leading to reduction in profits available for equity shareholders.

CAPITAL STRUCTURE ANALYSIS

The overall financial structure of an undertaking can be analysed as per:

(i) Duration of time
(ii) Trading on equity.

Duration of Time: The study of financial structure is done initially from the point of view of the length for which funds are needed with their respective ownership. As a matter of fact, an enterprise needs funds for financing *long-term, medium-term,* and *short-term requirements.*

Trading on Equity: It is analysed with respect to the debt–equity funding in the capital structure and the return enjoyed by equity shareholders.

Capital Structure Analysis of UltraTech Cement and Shree Cement

The present section analyses capital structure of the leading companies, *UltraTech Cement Ltd and Shree Cement Ltd* in the 'Indian cement industry' on a comparative basis. This will provide practical insights into the different financing policies of companies in the sector. UltraTech Cement Ltd is the cement flagship company of the Aditya Birla Group with highest market capitalisation in India's cement industry. Shree Cement Ltd was incorporated in 1979 and got listed in 1984 on Bombay Stock Exchange.

These companies are multinationals (MNCs) and listed, therefore their analysis will be relevant at international level. The data of the companies has been taken from 'Capitaline' (https://awsone-capitaline-com) and 'Ace Analyser' (https://www-aceanalyser-com) databases.

Indian Cement Industry

India is the second largest producer of cement in the world. It accounts for more than 8% of the global installed capacity.

India has a lot of potential for development in the infrastructure and construction sector and the cement sector is expected to largely benefit from it. Strong expansion of the industrial sector, which has fully recovered from the COVID-19 pandemic shock, is one of the main demand drivers for the cement industry. As a result, there is a strong potential for an increase in the long-term demand for the cement industry.

Aided by suitable government foreign policies, several foreign players such as Lafarge-Holcim, Heidelberg Cement, and Vicat have invested in the country in the recent past. A significant factor which aids the growth of this sector is the ready availability of raw materials for making cement, such as limestone and coal. The cement demand in India is exhibiting a CAGR of 5.65% between 2016 and 2022.[1]

Parameters for Analysis

- 'Debt to equity ratio' of the units has been analysed to study their *financing policy*.
- *Degree of financial leverage* has been further calculated to measure 'the level of financial risk' of the units.
- The correlation has been studied between D / E ratio and ROE or RONW to find the *impact of leverage on shareholder's wealth*.

1. *UltraTech Cement*

The financing mix of UltraTech is given in Table 8.1.

In the case of UltraTech, it can be observed that there is negative and little correlation between D / E and ROE. D / E has been continuously decreasing during the years under study, whereas ROE has shown a fluctuating trend. This indicates that the company has not been able to leverage debt properly in the interests of shareholders.

So, it's always better to choose the debt option if EBIT is increasing and higher than the interest component.

2. *Shree Cement*

The financing mix of Shree Cement is given in Table 8.2.

TABLE 8.1 UltraTech's financing analysis

Types	*Parameters*	*2019–2020*	*2020–2021*	*2021–2022*
Financial leverage ratios	Debt / Equity (in times)	0.42	0.32	0.19
	ICR (in times)	4.06	7.27	11.39
Shareholder's wealth ratios	ROE or RONW (%)	15.24	13.09	15.26
	EPS (Rs.)	189.15	185.20	245.00
Degree of financial leverage	EBIT (Rs. in crores)	6,923.98	9,170.78	9,091.46
	% change in EBIT		32.45	-0.86
	EPS (Rs.)	189.15	185.20	245.00
	% change in EPS		-2.09	32.29
	Degree of Financial Leverage		-0.06	-37.55
Correlation	–0.08	Negative correlation		

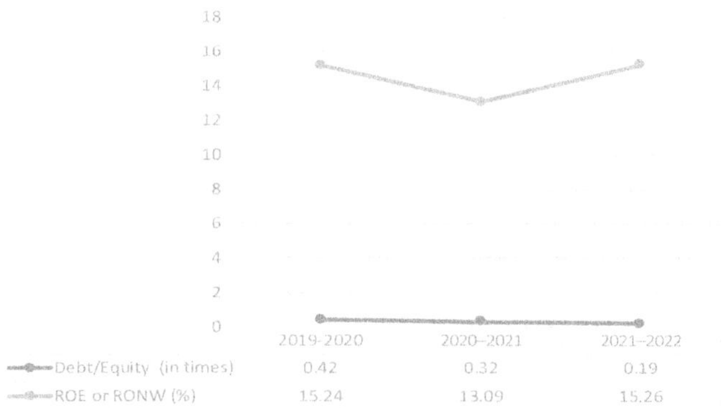

FIGURE 8.2 UltraTech's financing trend

TABLE 8.2 Shree Cement's financing analysis

Types	*Parameters*	*2019–2020*	*2020–2021*	*2021–2022*
Financial leverage ratios	Debt / Equity (in times)	0.18	0.11	0.09
	ICR (in times)	7.84	13.24	14.46
Shareholder's wealth ratios	ROE or RONW (%)	13.94	16.40	14.62
	EPS (Rs.)	445.08	640.77	658.69
Degree of financial leverage	EBIT (Rs. in crores)	2,246.73	3,272.82	3,148.70
	% change in EBIT		45.67	-3.79
	EPS (Rs.)	445.08	640.77	658.69
	% change in EPS		43.97	2.80
	Degree of Financial Leverage		0.96	-0.74
Correlation	−0.55	**Negative correlation**		

FIGURE 8.3 Shree Cement's financing trend

In case of Shree Cement, it is found that there is negative correlation between D / E and ROE. D / E has been decreasing for consecutive years but on the other hand, ROE has been fluctuating; first, it increased sharply in 2021 and in the same fashion, it fell sharply in the next year. In such conditions, it is difficult to establish the impact of leverage on shareholders' wealth.

Both companies have shown a similar trend, proving that leverage in practice might not favour shareholders' value. It could be due to other market conditions.

Reference

1. IBEF. 2023. *Cement industry in India,* https://www.ibef.org/industry/cement-india (accessed on 26 August 2023).

PART V

Dividend Decision

9

DIVIDEND POLICY

'Shareholders' wealth maximisation' refers to exceeding industry benchmarks in order to maximise returns to shareholders. Both capital yield and dividend yield are included in 'returns'. When a business consistently distributes dividends to shareholders in line with its growing surplus, dividend yield results. A business performing well and generating market returns to shareholders reflects a capital yield. The management decides on dividend payments, but they have no control over the company's performance in the market. Therefore, a suitable dividend policy is crucial for optimising the wealth of shareholders.

Dividend Policy: Overview

It is the management decision about the amount of profits to be distributed as cash dividends and the remaining profits to be reinvested for future growth. It also involves deciding about the payment in the form of stock dividends to the shareholders. The meeting of shareholders' expectations about dividends by the management influences determining the share value; therefore, dividend policy is a significant decision by the management of a company.

DOI: 10.4324/9781003730163-14

Forms of Dividends

The dividend paid by the company in various *direct* and *indirect* forms is as follows:

1. **Cash Dividend:** This is the most common form of dividend payment by the company. It is the dividend that is paid in cash in the form of final dividend or/and interim dividend.
2. **Bonus Shares:** 'Bonus shares' are also called 'stock dividend', as these are shares that are issued free of cost to the shareholders of a company, by capitalising a part of the company's reserves.

'Bonus issue' implies issues of 'extra' shares to existing shareholders. Bonus shares are issued to the shareholders in proportion to their holdings.

For example, the bonus issue of 1:2 means the company will issue one bonus share for every two shares held.

Bonus issue is a *'book entry'* because it increases the number of shares on one hand and decreases profits on the other hand. So, it does not affect the net worth in total. Post bonus issue, the share price usually falls in proportion to the bonus issue, thereby making no difference to the personal wealth of the shareholder in the short run.

3. **Stock Split:** A 'stock split' is a division of the stock into multiple shares with lower face value. It increases the number of shares in a public company. This is done by the company to make shares more affordable for the investors. It allows shareholders to enjoy higher dividends in the future.

In the immediate run, the price in split is so adjusted that the before and after market capitalisation of the company remains the same and dilution does not occur.

For example, a company with 100 shares of stock priced at Rs. 10 per share. The market capitalisation is 100 × Rs. 10 = Rs. 1,000.

The company goes for a 1 to 2 stock split. There are 200 shares now and each shareholder holds twice the shares. The price of each share is adjusted to Rs. 5. The market capitalisation is 200 × Rs. 5 = Rs. 1000, which is the same as before the split.

4. **Reverse Stock Split:** A 'reverse split' is the consolidation of the stock into fewer shares with a higher face value, and is opposite to the stock split. It reduces the number of shares in a public company. This is done by the company to increase the market price of share(s) for investors.
5. **Share Buyback:** 'Share repurchase' occurs when a company buys back its own shares from the market and reduces the number of shares outstanding. This is considered an alternative to the dividend payment as cash is returned to the investors through other means.

A buyback is a *'controlling tool'* which is used by the promoters or the management of the company to retain/increase control in their hands. Generally, companies buy back for probable takeovers or when they find their own shares to be undervalued or when they have surplus idle cash. Stock buybacks also increase the market valuation.

6. **Rights Issue:** A 'rights issue' is an issue of new shares to the existing shareholders in order to raise capital. As a matter of right, the new shares are first offered to existing shareholders in proportion to their current shareholding.

Procedure for Cash Dividend Payment

A company which intends to declare and pay a dividend adopts the following procedure. Further, if the company's shares are listed on the stock exchanges, additional requirements relating to 'listing agreements' are also to be followed.

Recommendation by Board of Directors

Dividends can be declared only on the recommendation of the board of directors of the company. The shareholders do not have any power to declare any dividend. The board of directors, after considering and approving the financial statements of the company, determines the rate of dividend to be declared and then recommends the same to the shareholders. For this purpose, a board meeting is convened to pass the resolution for:

(a) rate of dividend and the amount of dividend to be paid,
(b) book closure date for dividend purposes,
(c) date of annual general meeting, and
(d) bank account process for the purpose of remittance of dividend.

Approval by the Shareholders

The dividend recommended by the board of directors is declared by a resolution passed at the annual general meeting by the shareholders. The declaration of dividend should form part of an ordinary business item to be transacted in the notice of the annual general meeting. While approving the rate of dividend at the annual general meeting, the shareholders have the power to decide a lower rate of dividend than what is recommended by the board, but they have no power to increase the amount or the rate of dividend so recommended by the board of directors.

Dividend – 'Interim Dividend'

As per the Companies Act, 2013, the authority to declare and pay interim dividend is vested with the Board of Directors. An interim dividend, unlike a final dividend, can be paid multiple times in a year. Most companies tend to follow a practice of paying interim dividends on a quarterly or half-yearly basis, and their rate is usually less than the final dividend.

Dividend to be Deposited in a Separate Bank Account

The company should deposit the dividend amount (including interim dividend) within five days of its declaration in the separate bank account opened for this purpose. It means that the interim dividend will have to be deposited in a bank account within five days of the board meeting, whereas the final dividend will have to be deposited within five days from the date of the annual general meeting in which it was approved by the shareholders.

Determinants of Dividend Policy

An optimum dividend policy of an enterprise is determined after taking into consideration the following factors:

(i) External factors
(ii) Internal factors

External Factors

Following are the external factors which affect the dividend policy of the firm.

1. *General State of Economy*

The general state of the economy affects to a great extent the management's decision to retain or distribute earnings of the firm. In the case of uncertain economic and business conditions, the management may like to retain the whole or a part of the firm's earnings for future uncertainties.

2. *Capital Market Access*

In case a firm has easy access to the capital market, it can follow a liberal dividend policy. However, if the firm has difficulty in accessing the capital market, it is likely to adopt a more conservative dividend policy.

3. *Legal Restrictions*

A firm may also be legally restricted from declaring and paying dividends. *For example*, in India, the Companies Act 2013 and 1956 have laid down several provisions to be followed for the declaration and payment of dividends.

4. *Contractual Restrictions*

The lenders of the firm generally put restrictions or covenants on dividend payment to protect their interests. *For example*, it may be provided in a loan agreement that the firm shall not declare any dividend so long as the liquidity ratio is less than 1:1 or else.

5. *Tax Policy*

The tax policy of the government also affects the dividend policy. The management's inclination to retain a larger amount of the firm's earnings or to pay liberal dividends is guided by the tax factor.

Internal Factors

The following are the internal factors which affect the dividend policy of a firm.

1. *Desire of the Shareholders*

The desire of the shareholders cannot be overlooked by the directors while deciding about the dividend policy. The shareholders expect two forms of return from their capital investment, namely, *capital gains* and *dividends*. In most cases, the shareholders' desire to get dividends takes priority over the desire to earn capital gains because of the less uncertainty and sometimes due to the need for current income.

2. *Financial Needs of the Company*

The financial needs of the company may conflict with the desires of the shareholders. The management will give more weight to the financial needs of the company. However, retained earnings should be used as a source of financing only when the company has profitable investment opportunities.

3. *Nature of Earnings*

A firm having stable income can afford to pay a higher amount of dividends as compared to a firm with unstable earnings.

4. *Desire of Control*

Dividend policy is also influenced by the desire of shareholders or the management to retain control over the company. The issue of additional equity shares for procuring funds dilutes control. So, this factor also needs to be considered before arriving at a dividend decision.

5. *Liquidity Position*

It is also important for the management to take into account the cash position and overall liquidity position of the firm before and after the payment of dividends while taking the dividend decision.

Dividend Policies: Types

Various companies adopt different kinds of dividend policies. These policies are determined on the basis of factors, as discussed above. So, each of the dividend policies may exist across industries.

Following are the various dividend policies followed by companies.

Constant Dividend per Share Policy

In this policy, companies pay out a constant DPS irrespective of their EPS, that is a change in their PAT (whether increase or decrease) would not affect the dividend paid out to shareholders. This kind of policy generally is an indication of the fact that the company does not prioritise shareholders' payout in the current run.

This type of policy is usually resorted to by companies which have minimum growth potential and little scope for any large expansion. Table 9.1 and the respective figure present an example of such policy. Here, Apollo Tyres Ltd has paid a fixed amount of dividend of Rs. 4.50 per share irrespective of changing EPS throughout the years.

Constant Dividend Payout Policy

A 'constant dividend payment policy' means that a corporation establishes a certain 'dividend payout ratio' and applies this to earnings every year; that is, the fraction of earnings paid out as dividends every year.

This policy ensures that retentions as well as dividends fluctuate with earnings, but with given investment plans. In such

TABLE 9.1 Dividend policy of Apollo Tyres

	2003	*2004*	*2005*	*2006*	*2007*
EPS (Rs. per share)	33.05	18.37	17.64	20.39	27.14
DPS (Rs. per share)	4.50	4.50	4.50	4.50	4.50

Source: Annual Reports of Apollo Tyres.

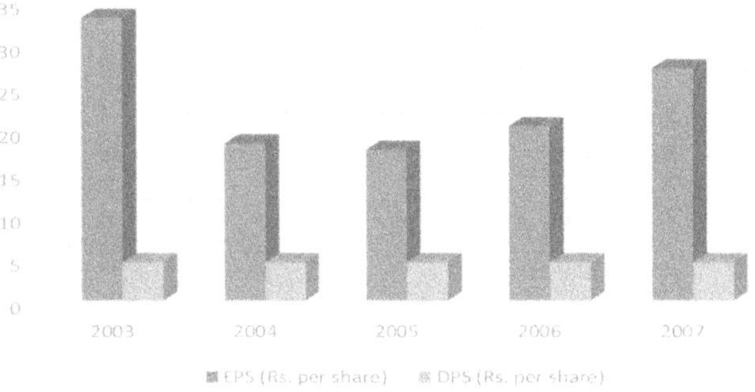

FIGURE 9.1 Dividend trend of Apollo Tyres

TABLE 9.2 Dividend policy of Bharat Electronics Ltd

	March 2011	*March 2012*	*March 2013*	*March 2014*	*March 2015*
EPS (Rs. per share)	107.69	103.74	111.23	116.45	145.90
DPS (Rs. per share)	21.60	20.80	22.30	23.30	29.20
D / P Ratio (%)	20.06	20.05	20.05	20.01	20.01

Source: Annual Reports of Bharat Electronics Ltd.

cases, outside finance will sometimes be required, and reserves are affected by the dividend policy.

Table 9.2 and Figure 9.2 present an example of such a policy, whereby Bharat Electronics Ltd (BEL), an Indian public sector undertaking (PSU), has paid a constant payout of around 20% throughout the time period.

Long-Run Residual Dividend Policy

A 'long-run residual dividend policy' is designed to give shareholders reasonable confidence in the payment of dividends. Such a policy is created by the corporation by *first* forecasting the relevant variables, such as earnings, investment needs, interest charges and taxation, for a given period, usually five years.

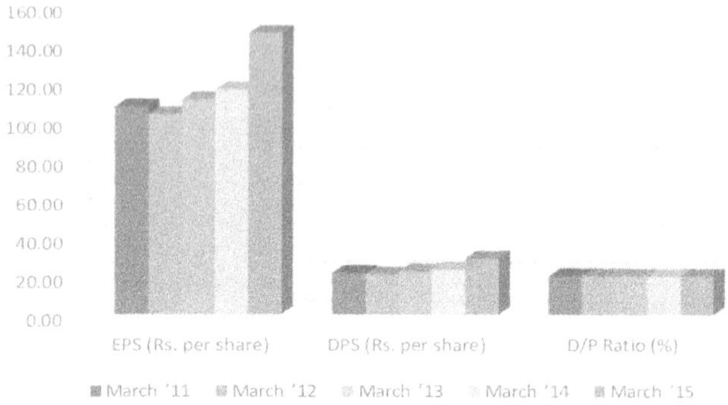

FIGURE 9.2 Dividend trend of Bharat Electronics

Then the dividends from a pure residual policy are determined, total dividends for all years are compared with total earnings over the same period. *Lastly*, an average 'dividend payout ratio' is determined. This is then applied to each year's earnings to fix the dividends.

Hybrid Dividend Policy

A 'hybrid dividend policy' encompasses a combination of the above policies as seen appropriate by the company. Using this approach, the companies view the debt/equity ratio as a long-term rather than a short-term goal.

As these companies generally experience business cycle fluctuations, they will generally have one set dividend, which is set as a relatively small portion of yearly income and can be easily maintained. On top of this set dividend, these companies will offer another extra dividend paid only when income exceeds general levels.

Dividend Policy of HUL and Dabur India

The 'dividend policies' of Indian fast-moving consumer goods (FMCG) sector leading companies, *Hindustan Unilever Ltd (HUL) and Dabur India Ltd* are analysed here to provide insight to the readers into the nitty-gritty of different types of dividend policies by different companies within the same sector. *These companies are multinationals (MNCs), therefore their analysis is relevant internationally. The data has been taken from annual reports of the companies.*

*Indian FMCG Sector**

The dividend analysis of the above companies is explained below.

1. *Cash Dividend*

(A) HUL

The company's dividend trend shows a 'constant dividend policy' with few exceptions. For the year 2011, Hindustan Unilever has declared a total equity dividend of 700% amounting to Rs. 7.00 per share. The company has shown a good dividend track by consistently declaring dividends for the period of the next five years.

TABLE 9.3 Dividend at a glance of HUL

Announcement date	*Effective date*	*Dividend type*	*Dividend %*	*Remarks*
17-10-2011	04-11-2011	Interim	350	–
09-05-2011	08-07-2011	Final	350	–
14-10-2010	01-11-2010	Interim	300	–
25-05-2010	08-07-2010	Final	350	–
15-10-2009	06-11-2009	Interim	300	–
11-05-2009	12-06-2009	Final	400	–
15-07-2008	04-08-2008	Interim	350	–
13-02-2008	17-03-2008	Final	300	–
23-10-2007	07-11-2007	Interim	300	Dividend (Platinum Jubilee)
23-07-2007	07-08-2007	Interim	300	–
20-02-2007	20-04-2007	Final	300	AGM
10-07-2006	08-08-2006	Interim	300	–
14-02-2006	28-04-2006	Final	250	AGM

*Refer to Chapter 6, 'Working Capital Management', for Indian FMCG sector overview.

Dividend Payout Ratio (%)

- For 2008–2009: 76.47
- For 2009–2010: 75.20
- For 2010–2011: 71.20

(B) DABUR

The company has a good dividend record and consistently declared dividends for the period of 2006 to 2011.

The board endeavours to maintain the dividend payout ratio around 50% according to:

(a) the company's need for capital for its growth; and
(b) the availability of adequate cash flow.

Dividend Payout Ratio (%)

- For 2008–2009: 47.41
- For 2009–2010 : 46.89
- For 2010–2011: 49.43

TABLE 9.4 Dividend at a glance of Dabur

Announcement date	*Effective date*	*Dividend type*	*Dividend (%)*	*Remarks*
14-10-2011	04-11-2011	Interim	55.00	–
27-04-2011	29-06-2011	Final	65.00	–
13-10-2010	02-11-2010	Interim	50.00	–
18-06-2010	03-08-2010	Final	125.00	–
14-10-2009	30-10-2009	Interim	75.00	–
29-04-2009	29-06-2009	Final	100.00	–
13-01-2009	02-02-2009	Interim	75.00	–
30-04-2008	19-06-2008	Final	75.00	AGM
10-10-2007	29-10-2007	Interim	75.00	–
05-03-2007	16-03-2007	Interim	75.00	–
09-10-2006	03-11-2006	Interim	100.00	–
25-04-2006	21-06-2006	Final	100.00	AGM

2. *Bonus Issue*

(A) HUL

The last bonus announced by Hindustan Unilever in 1991 was in the ratio of 1:2. This led to the quoting of shares ex-bonus from 19 July 1991.

(B) DABUR

1 The bonus announced by Dabur in 2010 was one share for each share.
2 Like HUL, Dabur has also been liberal in bonus issues during the period.

TABLE 9.5 Bonus issue of HUL

Announcement date	*Bonus ratio*	*Record date*	*Ex-bonus date*
30-09-1991	1:2	21-08-1991	19-07-1991
22-06-1987	1:1	–	–
22-06-1983	3:5	–	–
22-06-1979	1:3	–	–

TABLE 9.6 Bonus issue of Dabur

Announcement date	*Bonus ratio*	*Record date*	*Ex-bonus date*
26-07-2010	1:1	10-09-2010	08-09-2010
31-10-2006	1:2	29-01-2007	25-01-2007
24-10-2005	1:1	20-01-2006	19-01-2006
30-09-1993	4:1	01-12-1993	16-11-1993

3. *Stock Split*

(A) HUL

Hindustan Unilever had split the face value of its shares from Rs. 10 to Rs. 1 in the year 2000. The result was the quoting of shares on an ex-split basis from 3 July 2000.

TABLE 9.7 Stock split of HUL

Announcement date	*Old face value*	*New face value*	*Ex-split date*
05-07-2000	10	1	03-07-2000

(B) DABUR

Dabur India had split the face value of its shares from Rs. 10 to Rs. 1 in 2000. The effect on the share was quoted on an ex-split basis from 27 November 2000.

TABLE 9.8 Stock split of Dabur

Announcement date	*Old face value*	*New face value*	*Ex-split date*
03-11-2000	10	1	27-11-2000

APPENDIX I

Future/Compound Value Factor of a Lump Sum (FVIF/CVIF) of Re. 1, FVIF(i, n)

Period	*1%*	*2%*	*3%*	*4%*	*5%*	*6%*	*7%*	*8%*	*9%*	*10%*	*11%*	*12%*	*13%*	*14%*	*15%*	*16%*	*17%*	*18%*	*19%*	*20%*
1	1.01	1.02	1.03	1.04	1.05	1.06	1.07	1.08	1.09	1.1	1.11	1.12	1.13	1.14	1.15	1.16	1.17	1.18	1.19	1.2
2	1.02	1.04	1.061	1.082	1.103	1.124	1.145	1.166	1.188	1.21	1.232	1.254	1.277	1.3	1.323	1.346	1.369	1.392	1.416	1.44
3	1.03	1.061	1.093	1.125	1.158	1.191	1.225	1.26	1.295	1.331	1.368	1.405	1.443	1.482	1.521	1.561	1.602	1.643	1.685	1.728
4	1.041	1.082	1.126	1.17	1.216	1.262	1.311	1.36	1.412	1.464	1.518	1.574	1.63	1.689	1.749	1.811	1.874	1.939	2.005	2.074
5	1.051	1.104	1.159	1.217	1.276	1.338	1.403	1.469	1.539	1.611	1.685	1.762	1.842	1.925	2.011	2.1	2.192	2.288	2.386	2.488
6	1.062	1.126	1.194	1.265	1.34	1.419	1.501	1.587	1.677	1.772	1.87	1.974	2.082	2.195	2.313	2.436	2.565	2.7	2.84	2.986
7	1.072	1.149	1.23	1.316	1.407	1.504	1.606 1.714	1.828	1.949	2.076	2.211	2.353	2.502	2.66	2.826	3.001	3.185	3.379	3.583	
8	1.083	1.172	1.267	1.369	1.477	1.594	1.718	1.851	1.993	2.144	2.305	2.476	2.658	2.853	3.059	3.278	3.511	3.759	4.021	4.3
9	1.094	1.195	1.305	1.423	1.551	1.689	1.838	1.999	2.172	2.358	2.558	2.773	3.004	3.252	3.518	3.803	4.108	4.435	4.785	5.16
10	1.105	1.219	1.344	1.48	1.629	1.791	1.967	2.159	2.367	2.594	2.839	3.106	3.395	3.707	4.046	4.411	4.807	5.234	5.695	6.192
11	1.116	1.243	1.384	1.539	1.71	1.898	2.105 2.332	2.58	2.853	3.152	3.479	3.836	4.226	4.652	5.117	5.624	6.176	6.777	7.43	
12	1.127	1.268	1.426	1.601	1.796	2.012	2.252	2.518	2.813	3.138	3.498	3.896	4.335	4.818	5.35	5.936	6.58	7.288	8.064	8.916
13	1.138	1.294	1.469	1.665	1.886	2.133	2.41	2.72	3.066	3.452	3.883	4.363	4.898	5.492	6.153	6.886	7.699	8.599	9.596	10.699
14	1.149	1.319	1.513	1.732	1.98	2.261	2.579	2.937	3.342	3.797	4.31	4.887	5.535	6.261	7.076	7.988	9.007	10.147	11.42	12.839
15	1.161	1.346	1.558	1.801	2.079	2.397	2.759	3.172	3.642	4.177	4.785	5.474	6.254	7.138	8.137	9.266	10.539	11.974	13.59	15.407
16	1.173	1.373	1.605	1.873	2.183	2.54	2.952	3.426	3.97	4.595	5.311	6.13	7.067	8.137	9.358	10.748	12.33	14.129	16.172	18.488
17	1.184	1.4	1.653	1.948	2.292	2.693	3.159	3.7	4.328	5.054	5.895	6.866	7.986	9.276	10.761	12.468	14.426	16.672	19.244	22.186
18	1.196	1.428	1.702	2.026	2.407	2.854	3.38	3.996	4.717	5.56	6.544	7.69	9.024	10.575	12.375	14.463	16.879	19.673	22.901	26.623
19	1.208	1.457	1.754	2.107	2.527	3.026	3.617	4.316	5.142	6.116	7.263	8.613	10.197	12.056	14.232	16.777	19.748	23.214	27.252	31.948
20	1.22	1.486	1.806	2.191	2.653	3.207	3.87	4.661	5.604	6.727	8.062	9.646	11.523	13.743	16.367	19.461	23.106	27.393	32.429	38.338
25	1.282	1.641	2.094	2.666	3.386	4.292	5.427	6.848	8.623	10.835	13.585	17	21.231	26.462	32.919	40.874	50.658	62.669	77.388	95.396
30	1.348	1.811	2.427	3.243	4.322	5.743	7.612	10.063	13.268	17.449	22.892	29.96	39.116	50.95	66.212	85.85	111.065	143.371	184.675	237.376
35	1.417	2	2.814	3.946	5.516	7.686	10.677	14.785	20.414	28.102	38.575	52.8	72.069	98.1	133.176	180.314	243.503	327.997	440.701	590.668
40	1.489	2.208	3.262	4.801	7.04	10.286	14.974	21.725	31.409	45.259	65.001	93.051	132.782	188.884	267.864	378.721	533.869	750.378	1,051.67	1,469.77
50	1.645	2.692	4.384	7.107	11.467	18.42	29.457	46.902	74.358	117.391	184.565	289.002	450.736	700.233	1,083.66	1,670.70	2,566.22	3,927.36	5,988.91	9,100.44

Future/Compound Value Factor of an Annuity (FVIFA/CVIFA) of Re. 1, FVIFA(i, n)

Period	*1%*	*2%*	*3%*	*4%*	*5%*	*6%*	*7%*	*8%*	*9%*	*10%*	*11%*	*12%*	*13%*	*14%*	*15%*	*16%*	*17%*	*18%*	*19%*	*20%*
1	1	1	1	1	1	1	1	1	1	1	1	1	1	1	1	1	1	1	1	1
2	2.01	2.02	2.03	2.04	2.05	2.06	2.07	2.08	2.09	2.1	2.11	2.12	2.13	2.14	2.15	2.16	2.17	2.18	2.19	2.2
3	3.03	3.06	3.091	3.122	3.153	3.184	3.215	3.246	3.278	3.31	3.342	3.374	3.407	3.44	3.473	3.506	3.539	3.572	3.606	3.64
4	4.06	4.122	4.184	4.246	4.31	4.375	4.44	4.506	4.573	4.641	4.71	4.779	4.85	4.921	4.993	5.066	5.141	5.215	5.291	5.368
5	5.101	5.204	5.309	5.416	5.526	5.637	5.751	5.867	5.985	6.105	6.228	6.353	6.48	6.61	6.742	6.877	7.014	7.154	7.297	7.442
6	6.152	6.308	6.468	6.633	6.802	6.975	7.153	7.336	7.523	7.716	7.913	8.115	8.323	8.536	8.754	8.977	9.207	9.442	9.683	9.93
7	7.214	7.434	7.662	7.898	8.142	8.394	8.654	8.923	9.2	9.487	9.783	10.089	10.405	10.73	11.067	11.414	11.772	12.142	12.523	12.916
8	8.286	8.583	8.892	9.214	9.549	9.897	10.26	10.637	11.028	11.436	11.859	12.3	12.757	13.233	13.727	14.24	14.773	15.327	15.902	16.499
9	9.369	9.755	10.159	10.583	11.027	11.491	11.978	12.488	13.021	13.579	14.164	14.776	15.416	16.085	16.786	17.519	18.285	19.086	19.923	20.799
10	10.462	10.95	11.464	12.006	12.578	13.181	13.816	14.487	15.193	15.937	16.722	17.549	18.42	19.337	20.304	21.321	22.393	23.521	24.709	25.959
11	11.567	12.169	12.808	13.486	14.207	14.972	15.784	16.645	17.56	18.531	19.561	20.655	21.814	23.045	24.349	25.733	27.2	28.755	30.404	32.15
12	12.683	13.412	14.192	15.026	15.917	16.87	17.888	18.977	20.141	21.384	22.713	24.133	25.65	27.271	29.002	30.85	32.824	34.931	37.18	39.581
13	13.809	14.68	15.618	16.627	17.713	18.882	20.141	21.495	22.953	24.523	26.212	28.029	29.985	32.089	34.352	36.786	39.404	42.219	45.244	48.497
14	14.947	15.974	17.086	18.292	19.599	21.015	22.55	24.215	26.019	27.975	30.095	32.393	34.883	37.581	40.505	43.672	47.103	50.818	54.841	59.196
15	16.097	17.293	18.599	20.024	21.579	23.276	25.129	27.152	29.361	31.772	34.405	37.28	40.417	43.842	47.58	51.66	56.11	60.965	66.261	72.035
16	17.258	18.639	20.157	21.825	23.657	25.673	27.888	30.324	33.003	35.95	39.19	42.753	46.672	50.98	55.717	60.925	66.649	72.939	79.85	87.442
Period 1%	**2%**	**3%**	**4%**	**5%**	**6%**	**7%**	**8%**	**9%**	**10%**	**11%**	**12%**	**13%**	**14%**	**15%**	**16%**	**17%**	**18%**	**19%**	**20%**	
17	18.43	20.012	21.762	23.698	25.84	28.213	30.84	33.75	36.974	40.545	44.501	48.884	53.739	59.118	65.075	71.673	78.979	87.068	96.022	105.93
18	19.615	21.412	23.414	25.645	28.132	30.906	33.999	37.45	41.301	45.599	50.396	55.75	61.725	68.394	75.836	84.141	93.406	103.74	115.27	128.12
19	20.811	22.841	25.117	27.671	30.539	33.76	37.379	41.446	46.018	51.159	56.939	63.44	70.749	78.969	88.212	98.603	110.28	123.41	138.17	154.74
20	22.019	24.297	26.87	29.778	33.066	36.786	40.995	45.762	51.16	57.275	64.203	72.052	80.947	91.025	102.44	115.38	130.03	146.63	165.42	186.69
25	28.243	32.03	36.459	41.646	47.727	54.865	63.249	73.106	84.701	98.347	114.41	133.33	155.62	181.87	212.79	249.21	292.1	342.6	402.04	471.98
30	34.785	40.568	47.575	56.085	66.439	79.058	94.461	113.28	136.31	164.49	199.02	241.33	293.2	356.79	434.75	530.31	647.44	790.95	966.71	1,181.90
35	41.66	49.994	60.462	73.652	90.32	111.43	138.24	172.32	215.71	271.02	341.59	431.66	546.68	693.57	881.17	1,120.70	1,426.50	1,816.70	2,314.20	2,948.30
40	48.886	60.402	75.401	95.026	120.8	154.76	199.64	259.06	337.88	442.59	581.83	767.09	1,013.70	1,342.00	1,779.10	2,360.80	3,134.50	4,163.20	5,529.80	7,343.90
50	64.463	84.579	112.8	152.67	209.35	290.34	406.53	573.77	815.08	1,163.90	1,668.80	2,400.00	3,459.50	4,994.50	7,217.70	10,436	15,090	21,813	31,515	45,497

Present Value Factor of a Lump Sum (PVIF) of Re. 1, PVIF(i, n)

Period	*1%*	*2%*	*3%*	*4%*	*5%*	*6%*	*7%*	*8%*	*9%*	*10%*	*11%*	*12%*	*13%*	*14%*	*15%*	*16%*	*17%*	*18%*	*19%*	*20%*
1	0.99	0.98	0.971	0.962	0.952	0.943	0.935	0.926	0.917	0.909	0.901	0.893	0.885	0.877	0.87	0.862	0.855	0.847	0.84	0.833
2	0.98	0.961	0.943	0.925	0.907	0.89	0.873	0.857	0.842	0.826	0.812	0.797	0.783	0.769	0.756	0.743	0.731	0.718	0.706	0.694
3	0.971	0.942	0.915	0.889	0.864	0.84	0.816	0.794	0.772	0.751	0.731	0.712	0.693	0.675	0.658	0.641	0.624	0.609	0.593	0.579
4	0.961	0.924	0.888	0.855	0.823	0.792	0.763	0.735	0.708	0.683	0.659	0.636	0.613	0.592	0.572	0.552	0.534	0.516	0.499	0.482
5	0.951	0.906	0.863	0.822	0.784	0.747	0.713	0.681	0.65	0.621	0.593	0.567	0.543	0.519	0.497	0.476	0.456	0.437	0.419	0.402
6	0.942	0.888	0.837	0.79	0.746	0.705	0.666	0.63	0.596	0.564	0.535	0.507	0.48	0.456	0.432	0.41	0.39	0.37	0.352	0.335
7	0.933	0.871	0.813	0.76	0.711	0.665	0.623	0.583	0.547	0.513	0.482	0.452	0.425	0.4	0.376	0.354	0.333	0.314	0.296	0.279
8	0.923	0.853	0.789	0.731	0.677	0.627	0.582	0.54	0.502	0.467	0.434	0.404	0.376	0.351	0.327	0.305	0.285	0.266	0.249	0.233
9	0.914	0.837	0.766	0.703	0.645	0.592	0.544	0.5	0.46	0.424	0.391	0.361	0.333	0.308	0.284	0.263	0.243	0.225	0.209	0.194
10	0.905	0.82	0.744	0.676	0.614	0.558	0.508	0.463	0.422	0.386	0.352	0.322	0.295	0.27	0.247	0.227	0.208	0.191	0.176	0.162
11	0.896	0.804	0.722	0.65	0.585	0.527	0.475	0.429	0.388	0.35	0.317	0.287	0.261	0.237	0.215	0.195	0.178	0.162	0.148	0.135
12	0.887	0.788	0.701	0.625	0.557	0.497	0.444	0.397	0.356	0.319	0.286	0.257	0.231	0.208	0.187	0.168	0.152	0.137	0.124	0.112
13	0.879	0.773	0.681	0.601	0.53	0.469	0.415	0.368	0.326	0.29	0.258	0.229	0.204	0.182	0.163	0.145	0.13	0.116	0.104	0.093
14	0.87	0.758	0.661	0.577	0.505	0.442	0.388	0.34	0.299	0.263	0.232	0.205	0.181	0.16	0.141	0.125	0.111	0.099	0.088	0.078
15	0.861	0.743	0.642	0.555	0.481	0.417	0.362	0.315	0.275	0.239	0.209	0.183	0.16	0.14	0.123	0.108	0.095	0.084	0.074	0.065
16	0.853	0.728	0.623	0.534	0.458	0.394	0.339	0.292	0.252	0.218	0.188	0.163	0.141	0.123	0.107	0.093	0.081	0.071	0.062	0.054
17	0.844	0.714	0.605	0.513	0.436	0.371	0.317	0.27	0.231	0.198	0.17	0.146	0.125	0.108	0.093	0.08	0.069	0.06	0.052	0.045
18	0.836	0.7	0.587	0.494	0.416	0.35	0.296	0.25	0.212	0.18	0.153	0.13	0.111	0.095	0.081	0.069	0.059	0.051	0.044	0.038
19	0.828	0.686	0.57	0.475	0.396	0.331	0.277	0.232	0.194	0.164	0.138	0.116	0.098	0.083	0.07	0.06	0.051	0.043	0.037	0.031
20	0.82	0.673	0.554	0.456	0.377	0.312	0.258	0.215	0.178	0.149	0.124	0.104	0.087	0.073	0.061	0.051	0.043	0.037	0.031	0.026
25	0.78	0.61	0.478	0.375	0.295	0.233	0.184	0.146	0.116	0.092	0.074	0.059	0.047	0.038	0.03	0.024	0.02	0.016	0.013	0.01
30	0.742	0.552	0.412	0.308	0.231	0.174	0.131	0.099	0.075	0.057	0.044	0.033	0.026	0.02	0.015	0.012	0.009	0.007	0.005	0.004
35	0.706	0.5	0.355	0.253	0.181	0.13	0.094	0.068	0.049	0.036	0.026	0.019	0.014	0.01	0.008	0.006	0.004	0.003	0.002	0.002
40	0.672	0.453	0.307	0.208	0.142	0.097	0.067	0.046	0.032	0.022	0.015	0.011	0.008	0.005	0.004	0.003	0.002	0.001	0.001	0.001
50	0.608	0.372	0.228	0.141	0.087	0.054	0.034	0.021	0.013	0.009	0.005	0.003	0.002	0.001	0.001	0.001	0	0	0	0

Present Value Factor of an Annuity (PVIFA) of Re. 1, PVIFA(i, n)

Period	*1%*	*2%*	*3%*	*4%*	*5%*	*6%*	*7%*	*8%*	*9%*	*10%*	*11%*	*12%*	*13%*	*14%*	*15%*	*16%*	*17%*	*18%*	*19%*	*20%*
1	0.99	0.98	0.971	0.962	0.952	0.943	0.935	0.926	0.917	0.909	0.901	0.893	0.885	0.877	0.87	0.862	0.855	0.847	0.84	0.833
2	1.97	1.942	1.913	1.886	1.859	1.833	1.808	1.783	1.759	1.736	1.713	1.69	1.668	1.647	1.626	1.605	1.585	1.566	1.547	1.528
3	2.941	2.884	2.829	2.775	2.723	2.673	2.624	2.577	2.531	2.487	2.444	2.402	2.361	2.322	2.283	2.246	2.21	2.174	2.14	2.106
4	3.902	3.808	3.717	3.63	3.546	3.465	3.387	3.312	3.24	3.17	3.102	3.037	2.974	2.914	2.855	2.798	2.743	2.69	2.639	2.589
5	4.853	4.713	4.58	4.452	4.329	4.212	4.1	3.993	3.89	3.791	3.696	3.605	3.517	3.433	3.352	3.274	3.199	3.127	3.058	2.991
6	5.795	5.601	5.417	5.242	5.076	4.917	4.767	4.623	4.486	4.355	4.231	4.111	3.998	3.889	3.784	3.685	3.589	3.498	3.41	3.326
7	6.728	6.472	6.23	6.002	5.786	5.582	5.389	5.206	5.033	4.868	4.712	4.564	4.423	4.288	4.16	4.039	3.922	3.812	3.706	3.605
8	7.652	7.325	7.02	6.733	6.463	6.21	5.971	5.747	5.535	5.335	5.146	4.968	4.799	4.639	4.487	4.344	4.207	4.078	3.954	3.837
9	8.566	8.162	7.786	7.435	7.108	6.802	6.515	6.247	5.995	5.759	5.537	5.328	5.132	4.946	4.772	4.607	4.451	4.303	4.163	4.031
10	9.471	8.983	8.53	8.111	7.722	7.36	7.024	6.71	6.418	6.145	5.889	5.65	5.426	5.216	5.019	4.833	4.659	4.494	4.339	4.192
11	10.368	9.787	9.253	8.76	8.306	7.887	7.499	7.139	6.805	6.495	6.207	5.938	5.687	5.453	5.234	5.029	4.836	4.656	4.486	4.327
12	11.255	10.575	9.954	9.385	8.863	8.384	7.943	7.536	7.161	6.814	6.492	6.194	5.918	5.66	5.421	5.197	4.988	4.793	4.611	4.439
13	12.134	11.348	10.635	9.986	9.394	8.853	8.358	7.904	7.487	7.103	6.75	6.424	6.122	5.842	5.583	5.342	5.118	4.91	4.715	4.533
14	13.004	12.106	11.296	10.563	9.899	9.295	8.745	8.244	7.786	7.367	6.982	6.628	6.302	6.002	5.724	5.468	5.229	5.008	4.802	4.611
15	13.865	12.849	11.938	11.118	10.38	9.712	9.108	8.559	8.061	7.606	7.191	6.811	6.462	6.142	5.847	5.575	5.324	5.092	4.876	4.675
16	14.718	13.578	12.561	11.652	10.838	10.106	9.447	8.851	8.313	7.824	7.379	6.974	6.604	6.265	5.954	5.668	5.405	5.162	4.938	4.73
17	15.562	14.292	13.166	12.166	11.274	10.477	9.763	9.122	8.544	8.022	7.549	7.12	6.729	6.373	6.047	5.749	5.475	5.222	4.99	4.775
18	16.398	14.992	13.754	12.659	11.69	10.828	10.059	9.372	8.756	8.201	7.702	7.25	6.84	6.467	6.128	5.818	5.534	5.273	5.033	4.812
19	17.226	15.678	14.324	13.134	12.085	11.158	10.336	9.604	8.95	8.365	7.839	7.366	6.938	6.55	6.198	5.877	5.584	5.316	5.07	4.843
20	18.046	16.351	14.877	13.59	12.462	11.47	10.594	9.818	9.129	8.514	7.963	7.469	7.025	6.623	6.259	5.929	5.628	5.353	5.101	4.87
25	22.023	19.523	17.413	15.622	14.094	12.783	11.654	10.675	9.823	9.077	8.422	7.843	7.33	6.873	6.464	6.097	5.766	5.467	5.195	4.948
30	25.808	22.396	19.6	17.292	15.372	13.765	12.409	11.258	10.274	9.427	8.694	8.055	7.496	7.003	6.566	6.177	5.829	5.517	5.235	4.979
35	29.409	24.999	21.487	18.665	16.374	14.498	12.948	11.655	10.567	9.644	8.855	8.176	7.586	7.07	6.617	6.215	5.858	5.539	5.251	4.992
40	32.835	27.355	23.115	19.793	17.159	15.046	13.332	11.925	10.757	9.779	8.951	8.244	7.634	7.105	6.642	6.233	5.871	5.548	5.258	4.997
50	39.196	31.424	25.73	21.482	18.256	15.762	13.801	12.233	10.962	9.915	9.042	8.304	7.675	7.133	6.661	6.246	5.88	5.554	5.262	4.999

GLOSSARY

Accounting Rate of Return (ARR) (or average rate of return) It is the ratio of the average net income from the project to the average book value of assets of the project.

Aggressive Beta This is beta more than 1 and is more risky.

Aggressive Working Capital Policy It involves keeping a low amount of current assets by the enterprise. It finances the current assets by short-term sources.

Annuity If the same amount is invested every year, it is termed an 'annuity'.

Bank Finance It refers to the finance raised from commercial banks.

Beta (β) It is a measure of the volatility or sensitivity of a security's return in relation to changes in the return of the stock market.

Book Value per Share (BV) It measures the net worth to be enjoyed by the ordinary shareholders of the company after all debts are paid.

Bonus Shares Bonus shares are also called a 'stock dividend', as these are shares which are issued free of cost to the shareholders of a company, by capitalising a part of the company's reserves.

Borrowed Funds They refer to the borrowings of a business firm.

Capital It is the money contributed by owners. It is shareholders' funds in a business.

Capital Analysis This provides information about the funds required to start the project and keep it running until it is self-sustaining.

Capital Asset Pricing Method (CAPM) It is used to calculate the cost of equity, based on the 'risk-return' trade-off for securities.

Capital Budgeting Decision It pertains to investment in fixed assets/long-term assets whose returns are expected over a long period of time.

Capital Structure It is the composition of debt and equity. It is the total of the long-term funds of an enterprise.

Cash Cycle (or cash conversion cycle) It denotes the actual cash requirement to run the business operations.

Cash Dividend It is the dividend that is paid in cash in the form of final dividend or interim dividend.

Capital Work-in-Progress (CWIP) This includes under-construction or under-completion of fixed assets.

Cash Inflows These are expected returns from the operating activities.

Cash Outflows These are outlays that result from investment activities.

Compounding It refers to the future value of a present sum of money.

Conservative Beta (or defensive beta) This is beta less than 1 and is less risky.

Conservative Working Capital Policy In this policy, current assets are financed by long-term sources and keep a safety net for future uncertainty.

Constant Dividend Payout Policy A constant dividend payment ratio policy whereby a corporation establishes a certain dividend pay-out ratio and applies this to earnings.

Constant Dividend per Share Policy In this policy, the companies pay-out a constant DPS irrespective of their EPS, that is a change in their PAT (whether increase or decrease) would not affect the dividend paid out to shareholders.

Cost of Debt It is an explicit cost in the form of interest paid by the company on the loan amount.

Cost of Equity Capital (COCE) It is an implicit cost as there is no assured/coupon rate of return involved here. It is the rate of return that the firm must earn to meet shareholders' expectations and thereby increase shareholders' wealth.

Cost of Preference Capital It is an explicit cost in the form of fixed dividend paid by the company to preference shareholders.

Cost of Retained Earnings It is an implicit cost with no explicit obligation to pay a return. It is the cost of re-earning forgone by the shareholders.

Current Assets These are meant for current use, for day-to-day operations and are for less than a year.

Debentures (or bonds) They are known as creditorship securities because debenture holders are the creditors of a company.

Debt–Equity Ratio (D / E) It indicates the relative proportions of debt and equity in financing the assets of a firm.

Dependent Projects (*or contingent projects*) In this case, the acceptance of one proposal is contingent upon the acceptance of other proposals.

Discounted Cash-Flow Method of Valuation (DCF) It attempts to determine the value of the company by computing the present value of cash flows over the life of the company. It is widely used in capital investment decisions.

Discounted Payback Period It is an improved version of the payback method as it considers the time value of money.

Discounting It denotes the present value of a future sum of money.

Diversification Investment Decision It is deciding to enter into new lines of business either product-wise or territory-wise.

Diversifiable Risk (or unsystematic risk or internal risk) It is the risk that is controllable and can be managed by the firm, such as management policies, strikes, and so forth.

Dividend It is the amount of profits distributed to the shareholders as a 'return'. It could be an annual dividend and/or an interim dividend.

Dividend Decision It is the decision about distributing net profit to shareholders and retaining it for future growth.

Dividend Payout Ratio (D / P Ratio) It refers to the amount of dividend paid per share with respect to the earnings per share.

Dividend per Share (DPS) It is defined as the portion of a company's profit distributed to each common shareholder.

Dividend Policy It is the policy of the management regarding the profits to be distributed as cash dividends and part to be reinvested for future growth.

Dividend Yield Ratio (D / Y) It refers to the amount of dividend paid per share with respect to the market price per share.

Due Diligence It is an investigating process or audit of a potential transaction or deal so as to find out all relevant facts pertaining to the ensuing transaction.

Equity Shares (or ordinary shares or common shares) These are those shares which do not carry any special or preferential rights in the payment of annual dividend or repayment of capital.

Feasible Business Venture It is one where the business will generate adequate cash flow and profits, withstand the risks it will encounter, remain viable in the long term and meet the predetermined goals.

Financial Feasibility (or economic feasibility) This determines the commercial viability of the project, that is if its probable revenues exceed the total costs.

Financial Leverage It is the use of fixed financing costs by a firm to magnify EPS.

Financial Leverage Ratio It is the degree of total debt involved in the financial structure of a firm.

Financial Management It is the process of acquiring and disbursement of funds. It includes all the activities relating to planning, organising, directing, and controlling the funds of the enterprise.

Financial Structure It refers to the total amount of funds of an enterprise, both short term and long term.

Financing Decision: It refers to the process of raising funds from various sources.

Fixed Assets (or non-current assets) They are long-term resources, lasting more than a year, and are used for the long-term growth and expansion of a business.

Fixed Capital It refers to the investment in the fixed assets from the firm's capital.

Gross Working Capital It refers to the firm's investment in 'total current assets' needed to operate over a normal business cycle.

Hybrid Dividend Policy Using this approach, companies will generally have one set dividend, which is set as a relatively small portion of yearly income. On top of this set dividend, these companies will offer another extra dividend paid only when income exceeds general levels.

Incremental Cash Flows These are the cash flows that are affected, or change, if the asset is purchased.

Independent Projects The project whose acceptance does not affect the acceptance of any other project is an independent project.

Industry Analysis This analysis examines and identifies industry trends that are presently occurring in the marketplace.

Institutional Finance It refers to the finance raised from financial institutions, both central and state level financial institutions.

Internal Rate of Return (IRR) It is the rate of return at which NPV is zero; that is, the rate at which the present value of cash inflows is equal to the present value of cash outflows.

Investment Decision It implies the allocation of funds in various assets. The investment in fixed assets is called 'capital budgeting decision'. The investment in current assets is called a 'working capital decision'.

Leverage It is the employment of an asset or source of funds for which the firm has to pay a fixed cost or return.

Leverage Ratio This ratio is used to calculate the amount of fixed obligations involved in a company's structure and its ability to meet those obligations.

Long-Run Residual Dividend Policy Such a policy is created by the corporation by first forecasting the relevant variables, such as earnings, investment needs, interest charges and taxation, for a given period, and then dividends are determined.

Long-term Finance It refers to that category of funds whose repayment is generally for a period of more than ten years.

Market Feasibility It is conducted to determine the viability of a proposedproduct in the marketplace.

Matching Working Capital Policy (or hedging working capital policy) This policy is an arrangement where the current assets of the business are used perfectly to match the current liabilities. It is a medium-risk proposition.

Medium-term Finance (or intermediate-term finance) It is that category of finance whose repayment can be projected within a planning cycle of a reasonable length of time.

Mutually Exclusive Projects These are the projects wherein the decision to invest in one project affects other projects because only one project can be purchased.

Negative Working Capital It occurs when current liabilities exceed current assets.

Net Present Value (NPV) It is the difference between the present value of net cash inflows and the present value of cash outflows.

Net Working Capital It represents the difference between current assets and current liabilities.

Neutral Beta (or average beta) This is beta equal to 1.

Non-Diversifiable Risk (or systematic risk or market risk) It is the risk that is non-controllable and cannot be managed by the firm, such as interest rate changes, inflation, and so forth.

Operating Leverage It is the use of fixed operating costs by a firm to magnify EBIT.

Operating Leverage Ratio It is the degree of fixed operating costs involved in a project.

Operating Cycle It is the number of days taken by a company in realising its inventories in cash.

Organisational Feasibility (or managerial feasibility) It involves determining the managerial capability to undertake the project.

Payback Period It is defined as 'the time period required to recover the initial investment of the project'.

Performance Analysis This is the formal review process of the project with all parties involved at periodic intervals for achieving the desired results of the project.

Permanent Working Capital (or core working capital) It refers to the core current assets that are essential to run a business.

Positive Working Capital It occurs when current assets exceed current liabilities.

Profitability Index (PI) (or benefit–cost ratio ([B / C ratio]) It is the ratio of present value of cash inflows and the present value of cash outflows at the required rate of return.

Project Feasibility (or project appraisal) It is 'assessing, in advance, whether a project is worthwhile and therefore if it should be undertaken or not'.

Public Deposits They refer to the deposits received by a company from the public as loan or debt.

Replacement Investment Decision It involves a decision concerning whether an existing asset should be replaced by a newer one of the same type or with a different type of machine with the same operational use.

Resource Analysis This provides information about the operations of your business regarding the inputs needed to produce a product or service.

Share It is one of the units into which the share capital of a company can be divided.

Share Buyback Share repurchase occurs when a company buys back its own shares from the market and reduces the number of shares outstanding.

Shareholders Wealth Maximisation (SWM) Wealth maximisation is a combination of regular return to shareholders in the form of dividends and appreciating market returns.

Stock Split A stock split is a division of the stock into multiple shares with a lower nominal value.

Technical Feasibility It identifies the technical requirements of men, machines, and materials for the proposed project.

Technology Analysis This is assessing the type of technology required for the project and the constraints involved in the implementation.

Time Value of Money (TVM) It describes the relationship between the value of a rupee today and the value of a rupee in the future.

Temporary Working Capital (or variable capital) It is the extra working capital needed to support the changing production and sales activities.

Terminal Cash Flows These are the cash flows that occur only at the end of the life of the asset.

Term Loans These are long-term loans provided by central and state level financial institutions to the business firms.

Trading on Equity It is the ability of the firm to use debt financing to magnify the shareholders' return.

Weighted Average Cost of Capital (WACC) (or cost of capital employed) It is the total cost of raising the funds for investment purposes.

Working Capital This means 'the capital used to carry out the day-to-day operations of a business'.

Working Capital Management It is concerned with the problems that arise in attempting to manage the current assets, current liabilities, and the inter-relationship that exists between them.

Working Capital Turnover Ratio (WCTR) This ratio is used to measure the company's ability to utilise its working capital efficiently to generate revenue.

INDEX

Note: Page locators in *italics* refer to figures and **bold** refer to tables.

www.ingramcontent.com/pod-product-compliance
Lightning Source LLC
LaVergne TN
LVHW021130300926
849160LV00010B/948
9781041220107